MW00790362

Praise for the series:

It was only a matter of time before a clever publisher realized that there is an audience for whom *Exile on Main Street* or *Electric Ladyland* are as significant and worthy of study as *The Catcher in the Rye* or *Middlemarch* . . . The series . . . is freewheeling and eclectic, ranging from minute rock-geek analysis to idiosyncratic personal celebration—*The New York Times Book Review*

Ideal for the rock geek who thinks liner notes just aren't enough—*Rolling Stone*

One of the coolest publishing imprints on the planet—*Bookslut*

These are for the insane collectors out there who appreciate fantastic design, well-executed thinking, and things that make your house look cool. Each volume in this series takes a seminal album and breaks it down in startling minutiae. We love these. We are huge nerds—*Vice*

A brilliant series . . . each one a work of real love—*NME* (UK)

Passionate, obsessive, and smart—*Nylon*

Religious tracts for the rock 'n' roll faithful—*Boldtype*

[A] consistently excellent series—*Uncut* (UK)

We . . . aren't naive enough to think that we're your only source for reading about music (but if we had our way . . . watch out). For those of you who really like to know everything there is to know about an album, you'd do well to check out Bloomsbury's "33 1/3" series of books—*Pitchfork*

For reviews of individual titles in the series, please visit our blog at 333sound.com and our website at http://www.bloomsbury.com/musicandsoundstudies Follow us on Twitter: @333books

Like us on Facebook: https://www.facebook.com/33.3books

For a complete list of books in this series, see the back of this book.

Forthcoming in the series:

and many more . . .

Boxer

Ryan Pinkard

BLOOMSBURY ACADEMIC
NEW YORK • LONDON • OXFORD • NEW DELHI • SYDNEY

BLOOMSBURY ACADEMIC
Bloomsbury Publishing Inc
1385 Broadway, New York, NY 10018, USA
50 Bedford Square, London, WC1B 3DP, UK
29 Earlsfort Terrace, Dublin 2, Ireland

BLOOMSBURY, BLOOMSBURY ACADEMIC and the Diana logo are
trademarks of Bloomsbury Publishing Plc

First published in the United States of America 2022

Library of Congress Cataloging-in-Publication Data
Names: Pinkard, Ryan, author.
Title: Boxer / Ryan Pinkard.
Description: New York : Bloomsbury Academic, 2022. | Series: 33 1/3 | Includes
bibliographical references and index. | Summary: "Demonstrates how Boxer came at a do-
or-die moment for a hardworking, fiercely-driven group that has since gone the distance"–
Provided by publisher.
Identifiers: LCCN 2021047861 (print) | LCCN 2021047862 (ebook) | ISBN 9781501378010
(paperback) | ISBN 9781501378027 (epub) | ISBN 9781501378034 (pdf) |
ISBN 9781501378041 (ebook other)
Subjects: LCSH: Nationals (Musical group). Boxer. | Rock music–United States–2001-2010–
History and criticism.
Classification: LCC ML421.N37 B68 2022 (print) | LCC ML421.N37 (ebook) |
DDC 782.421660922/2–dc23
LC record available at https://lccn.loc.gov/2021047861
LC ebook record available at https://lccn.loc.gov/2021047862

ISBN: PB: 978-1-5013-7801-0
ePDF: 978-1-5013-7803-4
eBook: 978-1-5013-7802-7

Series: 33 ⅓

Typeset by Deanta Global Publishing Services, Chennai, India
Printed and bound in the United States of America

To find out more about our authors and books visit www.bloomsbury.com
and sign up for our newsletters.

Contents

CONTENTS

Author's Note

In presenting this book, I'd like to make a few things clear.

First, this telling is informed by over 30 hours of first-hand interviews with over 20 people. When trying to reconstruct the history of something that happened more than 15 years ago, you realize just how unreliable and conflicting memory can be. While I've worked tirelessly to corroborate the truest portrayal of what happened, this book inevitably contains some half-truths.

Second, when interviewing people, you learn that even the most eloquent speakers don't always make sense when their words are transcribed directly to text. For the sake of the reader and the speaker, the quotes contained within have been edited for clarity.

Finally, when writing about rock and roll, it's only natural to speak about a band as if it were a monolith, when in fact it's a conglomerate of individuals with different experiences. While I frequently characterize the mindset or feelings of The National in this fashion, keep in mind that "the band" in this story is something of a narrative construction based on my own interpretations.

Cast of Characters

THE NATIONAL
Aaron Dessner
Bryce Dessner
Scott Devendorf
Bryan Devendorf
Matt Berninger

THE NATION

Peter Katis: producer, engineer, amatuer hockey player; co-produced *Boxer* with the band

Carin Besser: Matt's wife and writing partner; co-wrote three tracks on *Boxer*

Padma Newsome: composer, arranger, and violist; Clogs leader; orchestration on *Boxer*

Thomas Bartlett: alias "Doveman;" longtime collaborator; keyboards and accordion on *Boxer*

Sufjan Stevens*: acclaimed singer-songwriter; piano on "Racing Like a Pro" and "Ada"

Alec Hanley Bemis writer and friend; co-founder and head of Brassland Records

Brandon Reid: live engineer, tour manager, and friend; "home recordings" on *Boxer*

Roger Trust: veteran A&R man and tobacco enthusiast; Label Head at Beggars Banquet

Mathieu Saura*: alias "Vincent Moon;" photographer and filmmaker; directed *A Skin, A Night*

Hope Hall: filmmaker and Obama campaign staffer; director of "Signs of Hope & Change"

Abbey Drucker: fine art and fashion photographer; shot *Boxer* album cover

Lizzy Goodman: journalist and indie rock historian; author of *Meet Me in the Bathroom*

Stephen M. Deusner: music critic and author; reviewed *Boxer* for *Pitchfork*

Brandon Stosuy: writer, thinker, and friend; reviewed early National records

CAST OF CHARACTERS

Matt Harmon: President at Beggars Group; head of marketing at the time of *Boxer*

Sonya Kolowrat: Director of Catalog at Beggars Group; publicist for *Boxer*

Miwa Okumura: Senior VP at Beggars Group; product manager on *Boxer*

*declined to be interviewed

Introduction

Boxer occupies a keystone slot in The National's story. Released in 2007, the band's fourth album was the first National record that many people heard, and within their beloved output it remains a cherished fan favorite.

A near flawless exhibit of the indie rock renaissance that blossomed out of Brooklyn in the mid-2000s, it's a puzzlingly smooth rendering of wide-ranging tracks that create harmony out of delicate songwriting, despondent post-punk, and lush classical arrangements.

Lyrically, it's a timeless meditation on love, depression, and adulthood that simultaneously articulates the hopelessness of George W. Bush's second term and foreshadows the hope and change of Barack Obama's meteoric rise.

For those reasons and more, *Boxer* is The National's easiest album to love, but it was anything but easy to bring into this world. Best embodied by its title—that great American allegory of the bruised and battered underdog who fights his way to the top—it represents a years-long struggle against popular indifference and mounting debt.

For onlookers *Boxer's* ultimate success cemented The National's transformation into one of the most critically-acclaimed bands of their time. For the band it was where their fantasy of being a real rock band became a reality.

While it wasn't their first win, nor would it be their biggest, *Boxer* is where The National truly became champions. But to grasp the full weight of that victory, you have to trace the band's rocky journey to get there: understanding their beginnings, their chemistry, their process, their mindset, and the people they added to their corner along the way.

This is the story of *Boxer*.

1
Twenty-Nine Years

When it comes to location, The National's origin story has always been hyphenated. Though the band was born and raised in New York City, all five members of the so-called "Brooklyn-via-Ohio" outfit hail from the hilly suburbs of Cincinnati.

Born in 1976, twin brothers Aaron and Bryce Dessner, grew up on the affluent east side of town, as did brothers Scott (b. 1972) and Bryan Devendorf (b. 1975). Born in 1971, Matt Berninger is the old man, the lone westsider, and the only one without a blood relative in the group.

The Dessners and Devendorfs all started playing music before age 10. Aaron played drums. Bryce got serious about the flute.* Scott and Bryan both started on the violin before graduating to the hardcore world of church-based handbell

---

*Bryce would break out the flute for the first (and last) time on a National record with the *Boxer* track "Racing Like a Pro."

choirs.* Everyone's worlds began colliding around 1988 when the sporty sixth-grader Dessners met oddball seventh-grader Bryan at the Cincinnati Country Day School.

> **Aaron:** Bryan and I had the same middle school adviser. He just was this weird, badass skater kid who didn't say much.
>
> **Bryan:** I was a loner. They were sort of the golden boys: blonde-haired, blue-eyed twins who excelled at sports and academics.

The first thing the three of them played together wasn't music, but basketball, with Bryan positioned at center and the twins as point guards on their school's B-team hoops squad.

Between the Dessners, Bryce was the first to get tired of being the short kid on the bench. Taking a cue from their punk older sister, Jess, who had jumped headfirst into the Cincy rock scene, he started teaching himself electric guitar.[1] Within a year, he joined the local conservatory, which in turn inspired Aaron to pick up the bass.

> **Bryce:** Our style of guitar playing comes out of me learning classical guitar and Aaron imitating me.

Meanwhile, as big brother Scott was getting good on guitar, Bryan was taking drum lessons from a guy named Steve Earle (no relation to the Grammy-winning singer-songwriter),

---

*In Bryan's case, handbells would prove surprisingly illustrative of his drumming technique.

whose band The Afghan Whigs was just beginning to bring some alt-rock honor to their hometown.*

When the twins found out Bryan could drum, it was on. In their first band together, Equinox, the trio would jam for hours on end, mostly covering classic rock standards like The Allman Brothers, Neil Young, and especially The Grateful Dead.[2]

> **Aaron:** We'd spend long, crazy amounts of time together. We wouldn't even talk much. We'd just be in each other's presence making a ton of music.

Meanwhile, the more misfit Devendorf brothers expended their harder-rocking tendencies together in a string of punk- and grunge-inspired groups that performed at various teenage house parties and contests.

> **Bryan:** We had our first taste of success when we advanced to the semi-finals at the biggest battle of the bands in town.
>
> **Scott:** We were eliminated when another band whipped out a grungy, pitch-perfect rendition of "Unchained Melody."

*   *   *

A certain Matthew Donald Berninger entered the equation in 1991, when, after studying pre-med and sculpture at a liberal

---

*Bryan swears Earle looked just like NCIS actor and 1986's "Sexiest Man Alive" Mark Harmon.

arts school, he transferred into the University of Cincinnati's rigorous graphic design program. It was on the first day of drawing fundamentals class that he found himself seated across from Scott.

> **Matt:** He laughed at all my stupid jokes so we got along right away. We pretty instantly became best friends in college.
> **Scott:** He was always the art director guy who wants to say a bunch of things, but he would be nice and include everyone.

Bonding over long nights and rigid critiques in the studio, Matt and Scott grew close to fellow design students Mike Brewer, Casey Reas, and Jeff Salem. After attending concerts by indie forefathers like Fugazi, The Breeders, Cowboy Junkies, and Paul Westerberg, the gang eventually threw their spare creative energy into a lo-fi garage band they named Nancy, after Matt's mom.

> **Matt:** Nancy was this drunken, embarrassed kind of rock, but I consider that a real band.
> **Scott:** We only played two shows. One was at a Greek restaurant and one was at a party in Casey's basement.

While Nancy never got past the garage phase, they threw together the songs and money to record an album before graduating in 1996. Then, with diplomas in hand, Matt, Scott, Casey, and Jeff moved to New York City to pursue their preordained careers in design, leaving their rock star fantasies behind them.

Despite shipping off to different universities—Aaron at Columbia, Bryce at Yale, Bryan at Case Western—the Equinox alums figured out a way to play in their second band together: a flowery female-fronted folk rock group called Project Nim, which incidentally featured yet another set of brothers in it.[3] A 1998 campus newspaper article described their sound as "Velocity Girl on Quaaludes" and "a less uppity Ten Thousand Maniacs [sic]."[4]

Aaron: It was a pretty terrible band.
Bryce: It wasn't cool, but it was weirdly successful. We would sell out to 500 people. We didn't even understand you could get a label, so we would just make our own CDs and sell them at shows. It was the first time we understood that you could make money playing music.

It was a Project Nim show at the Living Room in New York where the Dessners finally met their future frontman, who had come to see them with Scott.

Aaron: You could tell Matt was the coolest person. He had great taste in music, and was interesting and creative. It was like meeting a leading man in a movie.
Bryce: He was this handsome, super nice, charismatic guy. We'd joke and call him "Everybody's Best Man," because he'd been the best man at like 15 weddings.
Scott: He literally was the best man at my wedding.

Bryce: I remember Aaron being like, "God, if only that guy could sing."

*   *   *

When Project Nim reached its natural conclusion in 1998, Aaron, Bryce, and Bryan were living cheaply in New Haven, Connecticut, where Bryce was finishing his masters in music at Yale. Two hours south in Manhattan, Matt and Scott were working successful design jobs with a front row seat to the rock renaissance that was just beginning to spark on the Lower East Side with bands like Jonathan Fire*Eater and The Strokes.

Scott: Matt and I didn't really play music for three or four years, but we started to see these really good bands coming up.

Matt: I walked to the Mercury Lounge every day after work, and saw the first seven or eight Strokes shows.

Scott: We were like, *Wouldn't it be fun to try it again?*

It was the sweaty summer of '99 when Matt and Jeff Salem, later pictured on the back cover of *Sad Songs for Dirty Lovers*,* moved into a massive loft in Brooklyn. Located at the dead end of Bond Street, backed against the Gowanus Canal, it was a popular spot for people to dump trash and torch abandoned vehicles. While it was far from posh inside, as evidenced by the rats they called roommates, the loft's

*Scott's wife Liz is the face on the front cover.

spaciousness made it perfect for throwing big parties and, as fate would have it, making music.

> **Matt:** I think that space was one of the biggest reasons we started a band. It felt like that's what you should do with a space like that.
>
> **Bryan:** That apartment became our headquarters.

Bryce was off studying in Paris when Scott invited Bryan, who invited Aaron, to jam with him and Matt. United by their common affection for bands like Pavement, Silver Jews, Wilco, Yo La Tengo, Sonic Youth, Guided by Voices, Spoon, and Dinosaur Jr., the first jams were largely formless. Aaron was the fastest songwriter, often noodling out melodies on guitar or bass that Bryan and Scott, then acting as lead guitarist, would respond to with some understated magic of their own, as Matt scribbled out lyrics and started singing.

> **Scott:** There was no great direction or ambition as to where we were going with it. We were just trying to make something and having fun doing it.
>
> **Bryan:** The early jams were really refreshing: super mellow, easy feels, straight beats, easy to understand songs, and the lyrics were really good. It felt like, *This is different from anything I've done before.*

On top of beer, a key ingredient at those early sessions in Gowanus was the presence of Mike Brewer and Jeff Salem, who engineered the proceedings on Mike's Yamaha MD8, a piece of 1990s digital technology that allowed the band to create primordial multitrack recordings of their fledgling efforts.

Bryan: That was a big deal having Mike and Jeff there. We could play and then listen to what we did right away. It was instant feedback.

Aaron: We gave everybody a cassette to take home and it was already something where I was like, *Oh, I would listen to this!*

In no time Bryan and Aaron were moving to the city, as the loft sessions turned into an increasingly frequent social club. It was Christmas when Bryce got his first taste of what he was missing out on.

Bryce: I came back from France, Aaron had the tapes, and we listened to all of it. It was everything that we had not been able to do in Project Nim.

Early jam at the loft. (Credit: Matt Berninger)

From its casual origins, this untitled band wasted little time taking things to the next level, sometimes practicing two or three times a week and quickly amassing a songbook of original material.

> **Bryan:** We took it very seriously. I had this sense of naive optimism that what we were doing was worthy of attention.

After committing to play at an office party where Matt and Scott worked, they realized it was time to give themselves a name.

> **Scott:** Matt and I were riffing. We wanted to come up with something that was generic and didn't have a predisposed meaning, like the National Parks, the National Basketball Association, or NASA.*

* * *

By late 2000, The National had enough songs to record an album. While Bryce would sometimes sit in, he was primarily playing in a four-piece chamber group called Clogs, founded by his Yale friend Padma Newsome. His Yale connections would open several early doors for the band, including their first producer, Nick Lloyd.

---

*Their supposedly meaningless name would later backfire at a small gig in Germany, when a group of leftist squatters who the band was staying with mistook it as a pro-nationalist statement and boycotted the show. They also eventually discovered that music festivals have "National" brand porta-potties and rent-a-fences.

While you could rightly say that the first record was The National at its most aimless, there were plenty of things they had already figured out. Dripping of Wilco-inspired alt-country, the musicianship was tight as hell, and Matt's early American Gothic poetry was swaggering, sentimental, and playing with his persona as the intoxicated yuppie who bemoans heartache and trading daylight for a career.*

Adorned with a steamy photo of Bryan holding a wiffle ball while leaning halfway out of a timeshare swimming pool, The National's self-titled debut, which they nearly dubbed *White Skirt*, was released on a brand new label called Brassland Records.

> **Bryan:** I mean, it was "released" in that we put it out on a label that the twins started with their buddy Alec.
>
> **Scott:** The impetus was to give it some legitimacy.

When Bryce met Alec Hanley Bemis in college, Alec was a boisterous Westchester punk who published a zine and mailed around tapes. By the time the two moved in together in Brooklyn, he was getting his name out as a semi-successful music journalist—at one point writing a cover story on Elliott Smith for *LA Weekly*—but not enjoying the hustle. So he approached his friends with a proposition.

> **Alec Hanley Bemis:** Aaron had a finished National record. Bryce had a finished Clogs record. I wanted

---

*On "29 Years" he sings "You know I dreamed about you," a refrain that would eventually find a second life on the *Boxer* track "Slow Show."

Aaron, Bryce, Matt, Scott, and Bryan circa 2001. (Courtesy Alec
Hanley Bemis / @Brassland)

to be closer to music. Starting a label seemed like a
better way to do that.

Bryce: We each invested five grand to start Brassland
together.

While *The National* was technically pressed to CD by the
middle of 2001, their complete lack of distribution meant the
music wasn't exactly available. Writer Brandon Stosuy became
one of The National's earliest fans when Alec gave him a copy.

Brandon Stosuy: I went home, listened to it and was
like, *This is really incredible.* I made it my mission to
book a show with them in Buffalo, where I was living
for grad school.

To drum up hype for the show, Stosuy penned the band's
first-ever review,[5] calling the record "a chapbook of souls," "a
discarded Farmer's Almanac blooming with revelatory pencil
sketches," and "a stoic Bildungsroman penned in smoke."

In his 6.6 out of 10 review for then-nascent online
music magazine *Pitchfork*, critic Jason Nickey reduced the
band's "perfectly inoffensive adult rock" to a faceless Silver
Jews substitute while backhandedly complimenting their
musicianship and Matt's potential as a frontman, writing,
"Berninger hasn't found a distinct voice yet...but I get the
feeling he very well could someday soon."[6]

Even with no following, no shows, and no more than a few
CDs sold, The National had begun to take on a life of its own.
The music was good, and they knew it would only get better.

*   *   *

2
Underline Everything

New York City was a strangely exciting place after September 11th. With the wreckage of the World Trade Center still smoldering, two brewing wars in the Middle East, and a general fear about the future, there was a zany need to blow off steam and live in the moment. This environment would begin to set the scene for *Boxer*.

> **Matt:** People were just out trying to drown their anxieties and seize the night.
>
> **Bryan:** September 11th accelerated the darker stuff for me: self-medicating with alcohol and drugs, and just feeling a license to be young and dumb.
>
> **Lizzy Goodman:** The hedonism was very real, but it was fueled by panic. You felt like you had to jam all of the fun you were going to have for the rest of your life into one night.

In the early years of The National, the band was depicted as being made up of well-paid urban professionals who happened to make music together. In truth it was more of a sliding scale.

Alec Hanley Bemis: Honestly, the whole narrative of them having good jobs was probably me writing that, although in Matt's case it was pretty true.

Coinciding with the dot-com fuelled "new media" gold rush that centred around Manhattan's trendy SoHo district, Matt's eight-year career at Nicholson NY—which specialized in creating websites for big brands—saw him rise from junior designer at a firm of three employees to Don Draper-style creative director at a company of 120[1].

Matt: When I look back at it, it was amazing. It was like *Mad Men*, with the money and parties and awards shows. I was definitely writing from a person climbing out of that fast-paced world.

Scott also worked at Nicholson, while Aaron was down the street at competing firm Funny Garbage.* Bryan was a meagerly compensated fiction editor for Soho Press. Bryce was the starving artist of the group.

Bryce: I was teaching kids guitar, answering phones at Aaron's firm, and doing demolition for a work crew. Eventually my break was playing music for composers like Steve Reich and Philip Glass.

*In fact, Aaron was an assistant to Red Hot Organization founder John Carlin, who would later commission the Dessners to produce the *Dark Was the Night* and *Day of the Dead* charity compilations.

And while so many aspects of The National's rise were a brutal and humiliating struggle, the excesses of Matt and Scott's company presented certain advantages when looking for a space to record their second album in.

> **Matt:** The company was getting all this investment and expanding and hiring, so they took over the top floors of the Puck Building, which is an architectural landmark. My boss let us set up in the penthouse. It was this photographer's studio with skylights and a big whiteboard. That's when we first started using whiteboards as our master album map.

To underline this ludicrous environment for a completely unknown indie rock band, the penthouse shared a wall with Leonardo DiCaprio's home, while directly facing the apartments of Kim Gordon and Thurston Moore in one direction, and David Bowie in another.

> **Alec Hanley Bemis:** Matt is a convincing man. Like how the fuck do you get your day job to let you record your album at the most expensive real estate in Manhattan, across the street from Sonic Youth and Bowie? Charming motherfucker.

*   *   *

Tossing the Americana of their debut into a meat grinder of Nick Cave and Joy Division-esque post-punk, The National took a major leap forward on their second and darkest album, *Sad Songs for Dirty Lovers*.

Bryce: The recording of *Sad Songs* was vast and extremely
creative. There were tons of songs that we had collected.

This was in no small part due to Bryce's full-time involvement,
which turned The National into a quintet with two sets of
brothers in it. The presence of five strong and disparate
personalities, not to mention built-in sibling dynamics,
would test the band just as much as it fortified it.

Sad Songs also marked the arrival of two supporting
characters who would later have a fundamental impact on
Boxer. The first was a scruffy, eccentric Australian named
Padma Newsome.

An old-school composer—and Bryce's bandmate in
Clogs—Padma added a raw musical energy that was as
spiritually rooted punk as it was technically rooted in
classical, and over the next several albums he would be the
closest thing The National had to a sixth member. He also
brought an intensity to album-making that is best summed
up in his own words:

Padma Newsome: I consider collaboration a dark art.
If you haven't gone to a dark place, been changed or
challenged by the process, then you haven't actually
collaborated. Simply skimming a bit of classical
playing or instrumentation is not that interesting
to me. True work is a folding into and over, where
hitherto imagined outcomes are thrown away in a
kind of studio war or fast moving scrummage.

With Bryce and Padma filling out The National's grand
sound, the *Sad Songs* sessions uncovered exciting new

territory for the band. The tracks were also a thick, unrefined mess recorded by eager amateurs, which is where the second key character appears. In need of a professional to give their songs a much-needed shine, Aaron reached out to producer Peter Katis by recommendation of Brooklyn band Sea Ray. Unbeknownst to them, Katis had just finished recording Interpol's soon-to-be classic debut, *Turn On the Bright Lights*.

On top of his stone-cold mixing skills, his kind, ever-so-curmudgeonly personality, and his amusing obsession with hockey,* part of Peter's attraction was that he worked out of an old Victorian mansion in Bridgeport, Connecticut that he'd converted into a recording oasis for bands looking to escape the city. He called it Tarquin Studios.

> **Peter Katis:** They still had day jobs, so they'd come up after work and we'd mix until the middle of the night. It was brutal.
>
> **Aaron:** It was so fun! Sometimes we would take the train up, stay up all night, and then go back to work the next day.

As would become customary with National records, Peter saved the day on *Sad Songs*, using Pro Tools mastery and an architectural ear for song structure to make sense of the band's dense sound.

> **Bryce:** It sounded like a pile of crap when we took it to him. We were completely blown away when he would

---

*Do yourself a favor and check out Peter's hockey-themed novelty band "The Zambonis."

mix things for that record. With Peter you could suddenly hear Matt's voice in widescreen.

Peter Katis: Those sessions were really intense with painfully long hours, but I thought it turned out really well, and I liked the band. It felt like we had pretty good chemistry.

Aaron: We kind of learned how to make records with Peter. We would do a lot of work on our own, but then take it to him. He was the doctor.

Bryan: He's almost like a George Martin to us.

Over years and countless hours spent together under one roof, Peter and The National would create a humorous form of studio shorthand all their own.

Bryan: With Peter we speak a lot in code. If you make a wide-reaching judgment it's a "Stark Pronouncement."

Peter Katis: "House of Cards" means you do one thing to a song and it ruins everything, which was constantly true with them.

Bryan: If you say "Clark Bar," you're saying something sounds too cheesy, like a commercial jingle.

The product of brothers himself, Peter became deeply familiar with the combative sibling dynamic crystallizing within the band, often acting as tie-breaker or peacemaker when things got heated.

Scott: Peter has always been really in tune with us personally.

Bryan: We've been through it all with him in terms of butting heads and finding a way to get the mix.

The process of mixing *Sad Songs* also cemented the band's exhaustive approach to making albums, in which tracks are worked and reworked in every conceivable configuration.

Matt: After working with Peter, we started realizing that our idea of "mixing" the record was actually part of making the record. To this day it feels like when we start mixing we're recording as much as we're doing anything.

While inseparable from the intricate, nuanced music they eventually became famous for, this deeply time-consuming method would get them into trouble on more than one occasion, none more so than on *Boxer*.

* * *

Sad Songs for Dirty Lovers also marked a new level of seriousness for The National as an enterprise. In addition to securing their first manager—a sharp, savvy business woman named Dawn Barger—the band was approached by a small but hip French record label called Talitres, which offered to help release *Sad Songs* in Europe.

Brassland had also become a more legitimate venture after Alec Bemis secured CD distribution to help disseminate National records to those precious few who wanted them. He also hired a big shot PR firm called Nasty Little Man to do publicity, which gave the band their first splash of critical acclaim.

The band's first pro photoshoot. (Credit: Graham MacIndoe)

Their friend Brandon Stosuy wrote an effusive 8.4 review for the increasingly influential *Pitchfork*[2]. A writeup in *The Fader*[3] gave the band their first editorial photoshoot.* Nasty Little Man even landed them in influential music rags like *Rolling Stone*[4], *N.M.E.*[5], and *Uncut*[6], whose full-page 4-star write-up would prove especially persuasive in piquing interest in the U.K. While these reviews didn't translate into a massive swell of fans or sales, the band sensed they were onto something.

Bryce: I remember when we finished *Sad Songs*, I went into a bar and listened to it on headphones and was like, *Shit, this is good. Like, we're actually a good band.* I think until that moment, we didn't know we were.

* * *

---

*...while managing to misspell Matt's last name and credit Bryan as a guitarist.

3
Kitty Gets a Scratch

Like all great boxing movies, this one also features a love story.

It was Memorial Day 2003. With the day off from work, Matt and his pal Mauricio* caught a matinee of *The Matrix Reloaded,* which was shattering box office records that weekend. After having their minds blown at the cinema, the two bachelors headed to their favorite watering hole: a dim Brooklyn dive bar called Boat. Just inside, a beautiful, sharp-witted magazine editor named Carin Besser was already drinking with her work friend Meghan.

> **Carin:** It was around 4:30 p.m. There was just the right number of people in there for it to be easy to talk to strangers.
>
> **Matt:** We got a table by the front window, and right away saw these two women sitting over by the jukebox.
>
> **Carin:** I definitely noticed him as soon as he walked in. He was tall and gangly and just looked so nice.

*who shot the poolside image of Bryan on the debut.

Matt: She was hot. She had that kind of academic sexy about her.

After downing a couple Jack and gingers and drawing straws with Mauricio, Matt gathered the courage to walk across the room and ask the two women whether they cared to join them for a drink, which they politely brushed off. After another round, Matt was feeling bold and bloodbuzzed enough to give it another shot. This time he swung by and, in a comic, melodramatic fashion, asked, "Well, are you guys coming over or what?!" It worked.

Matt: Quickly after they joined our table, I realized this woman is not like the rest.

Carin: I just found him so kind when he talked with his Midwestern affect, and his point of view on things was really fun and funny.

Matt: I could tell how brilliant she was right away. She was an editor at *The New Yorker* and we talked about the books and movies and music we loved. She was this artistic kindred spirit.

Carin: Luckily or unluckily we were both smokers, so it was very easy to be like, "Let's go outside and have a cigarette."

Matt and Carin ended up drinking and smoking and talking all night long. Within weeks they were a serious couple, innocently embarking on their long journey as life partners and, beginning with *Boxer*, writing partners.

Matt: When I started sharing *Sad Songs* and the new stuff we were working on, she realized I wasn't some

Matt and Carin in 2003. (Courtesy Carin Besser)

dipshit hipster and we got excited about music together.

Carin: Our reference points and favorite songwriter-poets were all the same, especially Tom Waits and Leonard Cohen. I specifically remember us dissecting songs by Kim Deal, Cat Power, John Prine, Prince, and Simon & Garfunkel.

Matt: She was as obsessed with Leonard Cohen as I was. Many relationships have been built on that bridge.

*   *   *

Around the release of *Sad Songs*, The National's touring regimen would expand drastically, jumping from around 30 shows a year in 2001 and 2002, to nearly 90 gigs over the course of 2003.[1] A few years down the road, that figure would seem quaint.

> **Bryan:** We would book, schedule, and fund our own tours. We were a do-it-yourself band of brothers.
>
> **Aaron:** It was financially disastrous, but we were trying to find an audience.

With little to no fanbase, even in New York, the early shows were an unmerciful battlefield. In hindsight you might compare it to The Beatles' formative years in Hamburg. At the time, it just sucked.

> **Bryce:** For years it was sweaty punk rock clubs with shitty sound situations, often empty, playing early in front of other bands.
>
> **Matt:** We had an immense amount of anxiety and stage fright.
>
> **Peter Katis:** I'd gone to see them play at Maxwell's in New Jersey. It was not good. There were five people there watching, including me and my wife. I remember thinking, *I want to work with these guys, I actually believe in their music, but there's no way they could be a big band. They're just not good enough live.*

Playing to a completely empty room was a common enough occurrence that the band even coined a word for it: "0-fer."[2]

> **Carin:** I was visiting my parents in L.A. when they had a show in Orange County. I was excited to see Matt

after the show, and I remember getting a call early, saying, "I can come now because there's no one here."

It is a testament to The National's thick-skinned persistence that they were able to face, at best, half-empty rooms and halfhearted crowds night after night. That said, they weren't always doing themselves favors with their awkward stage presence and GAP store fashion sense.

Alec Hanley Bemis: They didn't look cool like Interpol or The Strokes. They didn't look *un*cool, but it was more of a cast of *Friends* kind of cool.

Footage from their most frequent testing ground, the Mercury Lounge, shows the band at peak ugly duckling phase.[3] With their eyes and feet glued to the floor, the Dessners and Devendorfs projected the enthusiasm of a funeral procession, as Matt clenched the mic stand for support, cigarette and drink in hand. While he hadn't found his frontman mojo yet, Matt's throat-splitting screams on songs like "Murder Me Rachel" and "Available" gave the gigs a dramatic high point.

Matt: The experience of touring around, playing to other bands' crowds, fighting to get people to pay attention to us, it was unpleasant. But we loved the songs, so we just put our heads down and held onto the music as the only bit of confidence we had.

To cope with the incessant rejection, the band was the first to make fun of their own flailing.

Early days at the Mercury Lounge, 2002. (Credit: Yun Rhee)

Bryan: Self-deprecation is not an attractive thing to
wallow in, but we do it amongst ourselves. To this
day we compare ourselves to a three-legged cat, and
then if something positive occurs, somebody will say
something like, "Kitty gets a scratch."

*   *   *

As opposed to the slog of touring everywhere else, one
wonderful, desperately-needed exception to the rule was
France, where The National found their earliest support base.

Brandon Stosuy: In the early days of dating my
wife, Matt sent me a video of them performing in
Europe to this huge audience. She was like, "Did he
Photoshop that?" because she couldn't believe there
were all these people into it.

With Talitres repping them overseas, the band got their first
taste of notoriety, and the excitable live crowds that go with
it. A full-page review of *Sad Songs* in French newspaper
Libération was instrumental in stoking the flame of their
Parisian hype.[4]

Bryce: With *Pitchfork* we were never "the band," but in
France we definitely were. They love little bands.

While it was anything but luxurious driving around central
Europe in a cramped van, playing smoke-filled bars, and
sleeping on couches for a couple hundred dollars a night, it
was the closest thing yet to the life they were dreaming of.

Bryce: People would just go insane. It was definitely the
first time where we started to think, *Oh, this could work.*

By the end of 2003, disc jockey Bernard Lenoir, regarded as
the French John Peel, was calling *Sad Songs for Dirty Lovers*
his favorite album of 2003 and inviting The National to
perform on Radio France.[5]

The band also became close with a young French journalist
and photographer named Mathieu Saura, who would soon
reinvent himself as a guerilla filmmaker under the alias
"Vincent Moon." Prior to gaining some renown as the
auteur behind *La Blogothèque's* Take Away Shows, and artful

documentaries for R.E.M and Arcade Fire, Saura would help define The National's visual identity on their next two albums.

* * *

With nine-to-five responsibilities complicating their increasingly aggressive tour commitments, the band began leaving their full-time jobs in late 2003.

> **Bryce:** I was teaching at a music school, but I was gone so much they fired me.
> **Aaron:** We had discussed quitting our jobs. We said, "In 10 months we'll be ready to do it." And then the next time we see Matt he's like, "I quit!"
> **Matt:** Suddenly the new media bubble burst, and I ended up having to figure out the next person to lay off, so I finally laid myself off.
> **Aaron:** We were like, "What the fuck! We're using your credit card to pay for the van!"
> **Matt:** I knew I could always go back to a job if I had to, so I wasn't that terrified about chasing this dream for a while, even if it meant living in a shitty loft, traveling Europe, and sleeping in youth hostels.

Of course, one of the great challenges of being an independent band without dependable income is that money quickly becomes the greatest hazard to your survival. Starting with *Sad Songs,* The National dipped into a long period of debt that they wouldn't emerge from until well after *Boxer.*

> **Bryan:** Matt and Aaron paid for almost everything.

Matt: Aaron and Scott and I would come back from touring and do freelance work for all the tech companies we knew.

Scott: Matt would often do the phone interviews, and over the years he had something like $5,000 in AT&T charges. There was this running tally of everyone owing each other money, and as we would make anything, everyone would get paid back.

Alec Hanley Bemis: I think Matt essentially financed *Sad Songs* to the tune of $25,000 or $30,000.

Matt: I don't really put money aside. I just throw it at whatever I'm excited about. I had had a pretty good salary, so I just poured it all into this band.

Alec Hanley Bemis: One of the things that kept The National alive in those early years was unemployment. Like, *Can I finance this tour with unemployment checks?* If that was illegal I think any statute of limitations has expired.

In a vulnerable moment when credit card bills posed the biggest threat to their longevity, the band was tempted by their first offer to sign with a tiny independent label called Thirsty Ear.

Bryan: They were offering us something like $15,000 or $20,000, which I incorrectly judged and said, "We should take this offer, because we need the money!" Everyone else rightly said, "No, let's wait."

*   *   *

4
The Band in the Sidebar

The National never fit into the New York rock revival of the early 2000s. Despite drinking at the same bars and playing the same venues as The Strokes and Yeah Yeah Yeahs, they may as well have existed on separate planets.

> **Lizzy Goodman:** If you were young in New York at that moment, you were not interested in subtlety, or depth, or class. You wanted to be smacked over the head with the most swaggery, sexual, unsubtle music on the planet. Anybody that didn't have that mentality faded into the background.
>
> **Bryan:** That leather and cocaine thing wasn't really something we could pull off. It was hard dealing with so much rejection while being adjacent to superstars in suits and leather jackets.
>
> **Matt:** I was probably self-conscious of not being that kind of band, but it also made me so hungry.

With neighboring bands blowing up all around them, it was hard for The National not to feel the pangs of envy and wonder if their moment would ever come. In particular, Interpol would unknowingly haunt them for years to come.

Bryan: We literally had a practice space next door to Interpol in Williamsburg. We could hear them play and I remember thinking, *Woah, that was good.*

Scott: We were in the same practice space, the same recording studio, the same producer. Their whole sound was so impactful.

Bryce: It was intimidating. You'd walk by Interpol getting into their suits to have photo shoots in the hallway.

Brandon Stosuy: Matt and I were getting a drink in the Lower East Side, and there was this really big *Village Voice* article about Interpol next to a tiny little sidebar about The National. Matt was like, "You know, man, we're always going to be the band that has the sidebar."

Lizzy Goodman: The irony is that Interpol tried for four years to get anyone to care, and no one wanted to sign them. So it's hilarious that just as Interpol was getting used to anyone thinking that they were a good idea, there was already a band in the rehearsal space next to them who's jealous.

* * *

Hidden in the shadow of their peers' success, The National kept on playing shows and writing music. In the cold early months of 2004, they joined Peter Katis at Tarquin Studios to record what ended up feeding their next two releases: *Cherry*

Tree and *Alligator*. In the band's greater story arc, these revelatory sessions represent the moment they truly found their sound.

> **Bryce:** *Cherry Tree* was when the music started to be more interesting. We started to be a little more ambitious in our style, and the ideas we were writing were weirder. We were allowing ourselves to follow our noses and see what happens.

Imagining The National as a big-top circus tent, they realized that when they posted up Bryan's mechanical drumming and Matt's emotive baritone as duelling tent poles, the rest of the band could more freely execute their various acrobatics underneath. The trick was to find balance between opposing elements.

> **Matt:** You've got me and Aaron's emotional thing. You've got Bryce bringing in these sophisticated, adventurous song structures. And then you've got Bryan and Scott with these New Order–Joy Division beats and grooves. That weird combination of flavors started to turn into something three-dimensional.

Mirroring this sonic evolution, Matt was also finding a new mode in his writing, eschewing the screaming seriousness of *Sad Songs* for tenderness and deadpan comedy on tracks like the sly, loving "Wasp Nest," the heartbreaking "About Today," and the epic monument to drunken confidence that is "All the Wine." Put together, the music and words managed to express feelings of sadness, joy, pain, and humor all at once. And it was unique.

Bryce: We were always trying *not* to sound like R.E.M., *not* to sound like Radiohead, *not* to sound like Wilco, Interpol, or The Strokes. Those negatives led us into some distant, dusty corner that was The National. It wasn't popular at first, but it was semi-original.

As fruitful as the sessions were, the band's increasingly obsessive approach was only extending the time it took to reach a desired result. When March rolled around, Peter had to show them the door.

Peter Katis: We recorded over a whole bunch of weeks in that winter, but I had to stop because the big shots, Interpol, were coming back for their second record, *Antics*. That was at least a three month interruption.*

After getting booted from the studio by the band that reminded them of their place, The National returned to Brooklyn and continued to work on *Cherry Tree* with Nick Lloyd. They also played a short run of shows with a different breed of rock stars who would show them the way.

Bryan: The band that bridged the gap between us and that Lower East Side thing, and really elevated the genre, was The Walkmen.

---

*The day before they had to leave, Peter remembers an inebriated Aaron having some fun at the expense of the well-dressed rock stars that were kicking them out: "Aaron gets up to walk downstairs, and goes, 'Interpol just called. They can't find their suits. Recording is canceled.'"

Despite The National's bottomfeeder status as the first of three bands on tour—at one point having to go on before doors opened when a fourth band was added—it was a eureka moment to witness The Walkmen in action.

Aaron: The Walkmen had a huge influence on us. We learned a lot from the intensity of their performances.

Bryan: Seeing them was a big part of learning how to fake confidence and not hold back.

Matt: The spirit of the comradery in that band was a model for how to be cool and classy. They were grown men and genuine artists at the same time. Most of our peers were doing some wild, clinging-to-adolescence

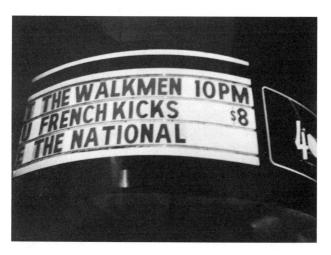

The Walkmen Tour. (Credit: Scott Devendorf)

vibe, but with The Walkmen we were like, *Okay, we're not alone out here. There's room for bands like us.*

* * *

The next pivotal character to arrive in this story comes in the form of a chain-smoking Englishman named Roger Trust. Since 1985, Roger had worked as an A&R for legendary British indie label, Beggars Banquet Records—the one-time home of Bauhaus, Gary Numan, and The Fall—where he'd signed acts like Buffalo Tom, Mercury Rev, Mark Lanegan, Tindersticks, and later St. Vincent. He was Label Head of Beggars when, at the tail end of 2003, a friend tipped him off about The National by mailing a copy of *Sad Songs* alongside a clipping of their recent review in *Uncut.*

Roger Trust: Unfortunately they had played in London just a week or so beforehand. As it turns out, that was a good thing as it gave me six months to get hooked by *Sad Songs for Dirty Lovers.*

By the summer of 2004, Roger was pining to find out what the band could do on stage. With about 70 people in attendance, he first witnessed them live at East London's 93 Feet East club.

Roger Trust: They were exactly the band that I hoped they would be, and I met the band and their manager Dawn Barger after the show.

Bryan: He was this big, friendly English guy who chain
smoked. His basic uniform was a black polo shirt
and cigarettes. He was very much at home in the
environment of a sweaty rock club. Such a lovely person.

Several days later, Roger went to see them play again in
France. Knowing he would be there, The National put on
an impassioned show, filling up the 380-capacity Nouveau
Casino in Paris with help from Mathieu Saura and his scene
of models, actors, and flâneurs.

Aaron: It was packed and sold out. Paris was literally
the only place in the world where that would happen
then. And we played really well. If you've ever seen a
good National show, that energy was there.

Roger Trust: The crowd was going crazy. The National
were fantastic. I was deeply hooked, and vowed to
sign them to Beggars Banquet.

After the gig, Roger and the band found an outdoor bar down
the road where they drank together until the wee hours while
dreaming up The National's bright future.

Aaron: It was really exciting sitting with him outside
afterward: a *real* English A&R guy from a *real* English
label with bands we loved on it. He was telling us that
we were going to be the next R.E.M., and we were
drinking in every word. It was one of the greatest
nights of our band.

Within a week Roger sent The National a proposal for a
three-album deal, and would remain their fiercest defender

through the label's merger with 4AD. It couldn't have happened any sooner.

> **Bryce:** Signing with Beggars was a huge moment for us. We probably would have folded if we hadn't. We just couldn't afford to keep going.
>
> **Bryan:** The key to our success was meeting Roger Trust. That's what saved us. He believed in the band and he didn't want us to change anything.
>
> **Roger Trust:** I had firsthand experience seeing bands benefit from an understated, word-of-mouth approach, and hundreds of others utterly destroyed by formulaic, cliched marketing and hyperbole. The National were an extreme example of understated and nuanced music, tugging at the heartstrings and soul of the listener. The goal was to make the band as successful as possible by treating the music with respect. The band deserved no less.

With the ink still wet on their new contract with Beggars Banquet, the seven-song *Cherry Tree* EP was released to mark the end of the Brassland era. Before it had dried, The National was back to work on their label debut.

*   *   *

5
The English Are Waiting

As the presidential race between George W. Bush and John Kerry was heating up in the late summer of 2004, The National got busy with their first album for Beggars—and *Boxer's* ornery little brother—*Alligator*, which was already half-done thanks to the *Cherry Tree* sessions.

Before inevitably heading back to Peter for mixing, the band set out to record some new material on their own. Inspired by his recent work on TV on the Radio and Yeah Yeah Yeahs' raw debuts, the band recruited new-on-the-scene producer-engineer Paul Mahajan to help record.

After recording the basic tracks at a local studio in Brooklyn, the band set up their own makeshift studio in Bryce's bedroom, located in the attic of Jess Dessner's house in Ditmas Park, where Bryce and Matt were both living. Aaron had also bought a house two doors down, turning the historic street into the band's new de facto home base.

Between the pressure of having to deliver for their new label, the nervousness of quitting their jobs, and the frightful possibility of another four years of George W. Bush, new tracks like "Secret Meeting," "City Middle," and "Friend of Mine" struck a decidedly more anxious tone, as did the most representative song of this time: "Mr. November."

Matt: That song was written about John Kerry. That idea of somebody looking in the mirror and thinking, *Yeah, I could be President of the United States.*

Carin: "I wish I believed in fate, I wish I didn't sleep so late" was the first time he took one of my lines.

Peter Katis: The line "the English are waiting and I don't know what to do" is Matt talking about how he doesn't know how the fuck to finish this record for Beggars Banquet. *He's* Mr. November.

It was early November, days after Bush's victory, when The National traveled back to Tarquin to mix *Alligator*. The results of the election cast a long shadow that extended all the way to *Boxer*.

Matt: Back then no one could believe that George W. Bush had won. I was so naïve about that.

Peter Katis: It was a dark time.

From the Brooklyn recordings, the band came proudly bearing a wealth of new material for Peter to hear. From a technical perspective, however, their audiophile producer was less than impressed with what they had captured on their own.

Peter Katis: I pushed up the faders to listen to the drum tracks and I remember Bryan saying, "We really nailed the drum sounds!" And in my personal opinion . . .

Bryan: The sounds we got were so anemic and just not rich enough. They lacked the necessary frequency range to actually do what Peter does with it.

Scott: Peter basically just told us, "Guys, you know I can't work with these. These are terrible." But we're like, "We love them!"

By the end of day one it was clear that a decision had to be made. As Peter was getting ready for hockey practice in his downstairs furnace room, he and Aaron had a serious huddle about how they were going to finish the album given the threadbare recordings they had to work with.

Peter Katis: I was packing my hockey stuff and said, "We've got to make a decision: Do we mix the record the way it is and see what happens? Or do we scrap these new recordings and re-record it?"

Aaron: He took me in the basement and was like, "Is this *really* going to be your first record on Beggars? Are you crazy? It sounds like a bad demo." We just had a feeling that it was right, so we stuck with it.

The ballsy decision turned out to be the right one. Using all the studio tricks he had, Peter was able to work around the rough recordings, which they balanced out with hi-fi elements and Padma's orchestrations. Not unlike the blurry Mathieu Saura photo chosen as the album art, they turned low-fidelity into something that sounded intentional.

Alec Hanley Bemis: *Alligator* sounds like it does, in part, because it was recorded like shit, and then Peter had to save it, but that's probably also where the charm of the record came from.

Peter Katis: This is a source of tension between us. They're so afraid I'm going to make the record sound too polished that it's intentionally made to sound kind of crappy. Their priority is to not be too slick at all costs.

In fact, the album's biggest showstopper wasn't even mixed or included in the track list when they left Tarquin Studios.

Finishing *Alligator* at Tarquin Studios. (Credit: Peter Katis)

Peter Katis: As we went to mastering, we ran out of time to mix "Mr. November." I said, "That song sounds like a mess." They said, "Don't worry, it's not going on the record." Then they put it on the record.

*   *   *

By the time the band's third full-length was released in April 2005, an encouraging trend was emerging.

The National was well liked by the dozen people who heard it. *Sad Songs for Dirty Lovers* garnered very positive marks, but hadn't gained them any traction. The reviews for *Alligator* were the best yet, and people were actually starting to notice, including indie rock critic Stephen Deusner.

Stephen M. Deusner: Artistically speaking, *Alligator* is the one that shows what they're about. That's their arrival. I like *Sad Songs for Dirty Lovers*, but the jump between those two albums is just phenomenal. That is where they went from being a pretty good band to a really great band. It put them on a lot more radars.

Pitchfork gave *Alligator* 7.9 out of 10.[1] *Billboard* called it "easily the National's best effort and quite possibly one of this year's finest records."[2] *Rolling Stone* was less impressed, summing up their sound as "depressed guitar poetry that's both elegantly wasted and kinda murky."[3] Their loyal fans at *Uncut* gave it a perfect score,[4] later placing it fifth on their list of 2005's best albums.[5]

To their benefit and chagrin, multiple reviews put them in line with a band they were all too familiar with being compared to. *Mojo* magazine said *Alligator* "walks the same Cold War-era Bowery streets as Interpol,"[6] while *E! Online*, of all places, called it the "sound of Interpol as reinterpreted by Tom Waits."[7]

Prior to *Alligator*, The National had yet to sell more than 5,000 copies of a single record. Before *Boxer's* release, it would sell close to 15,000 copies, essentially tripling their audience. It wasn't exactly Strokes numbers, but it was a breakaway personal best that minted them as a band to watch.

*   *   *

A month after *Alligator's* release, the band attended Peter's wedding in Greenwich, Connecticut. In between sets by the evening's cover band, a number of the musicians in attendance were taking turns playing on stage, prompting the guys in The National to step up to the plate.

As the Dessners and Devendorfs were picking up instruments, Matt grabbed the mic and cracked a joke about how they didn't have a lot of songs that were appropriate for weddings before opting to play "The Geese of Beverly Road" and "Daughters of the Soho Riots."

During the latter song, fashion and art photographer Abbey Drucker, who was then dating Interpol frontman Paul Banks, snapped what would later be chosen as the cover of *Boxer* using a small 35mm camera she had brought along for fun.

> **Abbey Drucker:** Paul and I were sitting to the left of the stage. I was having a cocktail at the time. I remember being mesmerized by the magic of The National as everyone started to dance. I took my camera and walked to the back of the room, knowing that it was

(Credit: Abbey Drucker)

a moment in time that I wanted to freeze. It felt like
a movie set out of the Fifties or Sixties. I took a few
frames and that was it.

Presiding over the sparsely populated dance floor, The
National looked scruffy, stiff, and unseen on the elevated
stage as dolled-up couples swayed to their elegant music
below. More than anyone could have known at the time, that
image of the band—playing to a half-emptied room of people
who came for somebody else—perfectly foreshadowed the
year to come.

*   *   *

6
Clap Your Hands Say No

Given that CD sales were in a rapid freefall by the mid-2000s, making a living depended on a musician's ability to cultivate a sustainable fanbase on the road.[1] With critical acclaim and a label in their corner, The National had their best chance yet to prove themselves. Over the course of 2005, the band became a touring juggernaut, playing a mind-numbing 133 gigs.[2]

> **Bryan:** That's when we first received tour support from the label. You know, that "free money" that you have to pay back.

Not only was The National headlining small rock clubs on both sides of the Atlantic, but thanks to the lessons of The Walkmen, they had metamorphosed into a live force to be reckoned with. For anyone who'd seen them in the early days, the contrast was striking.

> **Peter Katis:** I saw them several times over those years, and each time it got better. At the very end of the

Alligator tour, I literally said to them after a show, "Oh my God, you're finally good! You're *really* good."

With the band playing with the precision of a Swiss watch, and Padma Newsome adding a mystical layer of strings and keys in their live format, Matt had emerged as a physically commanding frontman. Keeping a bottle of wine by his side, which muzzled his stage fright while doubling as a handy prop, the audience had something to look at as he swung between rousing screamers like "Abel" and goosebump-inducing ballads like "About Today" like Dr. Jekyll and Mr. Hyde.

Unleashing *Alligator* in France, with Mathieu Saura filming. (Courtesy Alec Hanley Bemis / @Brassland)

CLAP YOUR HANDS SAY NO

Another major factor in the band's improvement arrived in the form of a long-haired, straight-talking, tatted-up twenty-five-year-old sound engineer named Brandon Reid, who was working the boards at legendary Philly rock club The Khyber Pass when The National played there in June 2005. From day one Reid had an intuitive knack for engineering the band's tricky sound.

Brandon Reid: From a live sound perspective, The National has always been a specific challenge, the main reason being that Matt's vocal output is really low when he's singing in his baritone. You have to deal with his voice in a specific way for it to even be audible over the band.

Aaron: We had just played in New York and the sound was terrible. Padma's violin would feedback every night and Matt couldn't hear himself. Beggars had just told us we needed a sound guy, and Brandon was so diplomatic and made it all really mellow and smooth. We were like, *Should we just get that guy?*

Bryce: At the time we could barely pay for it. I remember having an argument with my brother about it because he was like, "We can't afford it." And I'm like, "We *have* to do it, because this situation is brutal and we need to sound good."

Brandon Reid: They basically hired me on the spot.

Aaron: He literally jumped in the van.

*   *   *

Just two and a half months after *Alligator* hit record stores, another Brooklyn quintet known by the unwieldy name of Clap Your Hands Say Yeah dropped their debut album. Self-recorded, self-released, and holding the hypnotic earworm "The Skin of My Yellow Country Teeth," *Clap Your Hands Say Yeah* was a zeitgeist record of indie bubblegum that would demonstrate just how far an independent band could go without label support or radio airplay in 2005.

At a moment when everyone was thirsting for the next Arcade Fire, the record spread like wildfire on the dry kindling of MP3 blogs before exploding the propane tank that is *Pitchfork*, which awarded the album a sensational score of 9.0 and their game-changing "Best New Music" badge.[3]

> **Brandon Stosuy:** *Pitchfork* used to be a different monster, where you could get a review that would change you overnight. It was this weird moment where we were still so unprofessional, but had a lot of sway.
>
> **Lizzy Goodman:** *Pitchfork* became the most important arbiter of whether you were good or not. There was this perception of them being part of the new blog culture, where you were breaking down barriers between fan and artist without the traditional gatekeepers, which is funny because they *were* the gatekeepers.

Practically overnight, Clap Your Hands Say Yeah became the most talked about indie band of the year. It was an exciting success story that fed into itself, validating the futuristic new ecosystem that the internet had created. Things only got more out of hand when the bloggerazzi spotted influential figures like David Byrne and David Bowie at their first NYC shows. By the end of the year, "The Skin of My Yellow Country Teeth" would appear in an episode of *The Office,* and the album would sell 90,000 copies before even being released outside the U.S.[4]

> **Brandon Reid:** That was definitely the height of *Pitchfork's* ability to tell the public what they should care about. It was this insane vertical leap to public relevance.

With both Brooklyn bands buzzing from their recent albums, it seemed like a perfect fit when Clap Your Hands Say Yeah was invited to open for The National's biggest North American tour yet, which quickly sold out. It wasn't until the shows started in the fall that The National learned who many ticket holders were coming to see.

> **Aaron:** Very quickly there was this weird phenomenon where our shows would sell out with people who had no idea who we were. They would densely pack into these sweaty, small venues and watch Clap Your Hands, and by the time we'd get on stage it'd sometimes be nearly empty.
>
> **Alec Hanley Bemis:** It was awkward as shit!
>
> **Carin:** I have this vivid image of them all joking around, but in so much pain over it. It was so painful.

Luckily for The National, years of trying to win over half-empty bars had prepared them for this. In his *Pitchfork* review of their Philadelphia gig, Stephen Deusner noted that "maybe half the crowd left after the first set," while admirably quipping, "Whether those deserters were sheepishly obeying the current indie fad is debatable, but it's their loss: They missed the better of the two bands."[5]

Stephen M. Deusner: The National was *really* good. When the place emptied out it was very obvious, but it didn't seem like they were playing with any kind of disappointment.

The vexing trend of crowds coming to see Clap Your Hands Say Yeah and then emptying out before The National could play a note became a nightly occurrence. And it led to some spirited debates on the blogosphere, which generally boiled down to the consensus that Clap Your Hands was horribly overrated and The National was criminally underrated.[6]

Lizzy Goodman: It was the big moment where people talking shit about what they love and hate through their keyboards became the new journalism of the era, and that had its pluses and minuses.

Bryce: It was annoying and frustrating that that was the story being told about us at the time.

Eventually the band managed to stanch the bleeding.

Aaron: It was a painful process, but as we went across the country, it got better. We realized that we had to play so well. We'd get up there and start playing as quickly as we could to try to keep people in the room, and it did work. We always had to figure out how to win people over.

Unfortunately, critical praise and strong performances couldn't change the popular tide, creating an awkward financial situation where, as the headliner, The National was making the majority of money from the ticket sales their support act was driving.

Brandon Reid: When it became abundantly clear that the majority of the public was packing the room to see Clap Your Hands, there started to be some conversations between the bands and their respective booking agents.

Out of fairness, a decision was made: the two bands would split their profits, and Clap Your Hands would take the headlining slot for the majority of their remaining shows. While the economic undercut certainly stung, the deflating blow of being demoted to supporting act was worse.

Bryce: We would end with "Mr. November" and everybody was just waiting for us to get offstage.

With less than 40 minutes of released material up their sleeves, and backlash against them, Clap Your Hands didn't necessarily thrive on top of the bill. In his vicious live writeup for Vancouver weekly *The Georgia Straight*, Adrian Mack sympathized with The National's "public wedgie" while pointing to Clap Your Hands Say Yeah's lackluster headlining set as evidence that "a certain type of student with a hard-on for *Vice* magazine will fall for anything that comes from New York (except for the National)."[7]

Matt: I don't think it was a backlash against them, it was a backlash against hype. Poor Clap Your Hands, they had a ridiculous ride that didn't really have much to do with them.

Eventually the whole saga turned into a running joke in the blogosphere. After The National performed at the second annual PLUG Independent Music Awards, where Clap Your Hands won Best New Artist, a *Brooklyn Vegan* headline recapping the night read: "I stayed for the National."[8]

The always self-deprecating National crew even got in on it when they organized a semi-competitive soccer game between the two bands. Wearing their respective merch table T-shirts as jerseys, their website later billed the rumble in the park as the "Indie Rock 'Football' Showdown 2005,"

Indie Rock "Football" Showdown 2005. (Credit: Lisa Molinaro)

complete with a dramatic photo gallery of the event.[9] And at least on this occasion, they won the match.

> **Bryan:** We kind of embraced the Bad News Bears mentality of it. And the Clap Your Hands guys remain friends. Besides the humiliation of being relegated, it was pretty fun.

Ultimately the so-called controversy had an unforeseen benefit for The National, who were suddenly noticing an uptick in their audiences after parting ways to tour Europe.

> **Bryce:** I remember the show in London being much bigger than anything we had done before. So as the year went on, we kind of started to look at it as a good thing. More people had heard of The National because of it.

Even so, the ordeal left a permanent scar on the band's battered psyche. After years of similarly humiliating experiences, they were seriously questioning how long they could keep fighting.

> **Matt:** The Clap Your Hands tour was sort of a defining thing for us. If we'd had another eat-your-shit failure, we probably would have been dropped.
>
> **Scott:** Deservedly so.
>
> **Brandon Reid:** That scenario underscored how competitive the indie rock landscape was at the time. I feel like the Dessners specifically knew that if they

didn't put a record out that equaled or bettered the critical acclaim of *Alligator*, they'd be toast.

Aaron: Yet again, we were in a spot where we had to prove ourselves.

*   *   *

7
Don't Get Stuck in a Corner

After thoroughly wearing themselves out on the road, The National began writing material for *Boxer* in the early months of 2006. In their minds, the stakes had never been higher.

Carin: I was working around a lot of writers and book editors, and there was this thing where they would talk about a writer by saying something like, "So they're working on their second book . . ." There was this "uh oh" way about it, where everyone knew that the second one was harder to conceive and had to be somehow more significant.

Bryan: I remember a feeling of immense pressure and anxiety going into *Boxer*.

Scott: It was our legitimate sophomore effort for the label, which we had a lot of respect for. We were under the pressure of trying to make the follow-up to a thing that got us signed.

Matt: It was the first time we were taken seriously. People were going to be really paying attention to this record. *Alligator* got us in the door; *Boxer* had to be the one to show we weren't just one of those flash-in-the-pan bands.

Piled on top of the creative expectations they were feeling, financial, practical, and emotional concerns had mounted to a near-breaking point within the band. After seven years of trying to punch their way up, the cracks were showing. They were still cramming into a tour van for more than half the year, still in debt, still freelancing and leaning on wives and girlfriends to pay the bills, and they knew they could only fight for so much longer. This album represented their last best chance to make things work.

> **Bryce:** We were definitely still in survival mode. We'd lost our jobs and were having to tour all the time. There were questions of: *Can we really make a living like this? Can we even keep going like this?*
>
> **Peter Katis:** They felt a lot of pressure. There was even talk of, *If this record doesn't go anywhere, then that's it.*

To add to the above pressures on the band, their lead music writer was going through a personal battle all his own, intensified by the unraveling of his marriage.

> **Aaron:** I've struggled with depression my whole adult life, off and on. I was in a pretty dark spot, and confused about a lot of things. I had moved out of the house I'd been living in with my first wife. I was like, *What am I doing? What have I done?*

To a certain degree this precarious emotional state influenced the sound of *Boxer* from the absolute beginning.

Aaron: I was staying with one of my oldest friends, sleeping in his living room, which is where I wrote a lot of ideas for *Boxer*, and sketched out songs like "Gospel," "Start a War," and "Slow Show."

With no guarantee there was going to be another go-round, The National knew this record had to be bigger and better than *Alligator*. It had to be the best thing they'd ever done.

Matt: Everybody was really ambitious. None of us wanted to be that band that had that one record. And so Bryce was bringing a lot. Bryan and Scott were bringing it. Aaron was always bringing his best game.

Bryce: I was always wanting to shake things up. We had done it a bit on *Alligator*, but on *Boxer* we had to be even more ambitious

When it came to how this new album should sound, the moderate success of *Alligator* posed a new vulnerability the ever self-aware band had to consider. With eyes and ears now on them, they were keenly aware people would be comparing their new album to the last one.

Carin: It had to follow up the first bit of attention they had gotten. It couldn't just be anything. It felt like it had to satisfy some expectation, but they'd never had to write for a base of listeners before.

Aaron: We were in a very creative time, but we were still figuring out the ingredients that would flourish in our rock band. We knew instinctively we had to pivot somehow.

Matt: I was really nervous about getting stuck in a
corner. Early on we saw ourselves almost getting
stuck in that Americana corner, so *Boxer* was very
much like, *Let's not be any 'kind' of band.* We didn't
even want to be the kind of band that made *Alligator.*
Avoiding those kinds of traps was always a big
motivator for us.

*   *   *

One thing that The National had going for them was that
they weren't entirely alone anymore.

While on tour they'd met indie it-band Arcade Fire, who
became strong supporters of what they were doing.* And
after feeling like invisible outcasts to Lower East Side giants
like Interpol and The Strokes, they were at the center of a
new wave of like-minded Brooklyn bands like Grizzly Bear,
Animal Collective, and, yes, Clap Your Hands Say Yeah.

Aaron: It became this close-knit community that started
to feel like a scene. There were a lot of musicians
living around us in Ditmas Park. If you wanted
trombone on your record, there was a world-class
trombone player around the corner.

Most consequentially, Sufjan Stevens, himself a Midwestern
transplant who Bryce first met in the early 2000s after Sufjan
attended the early Clogs shows, had literally moved down the

*Bryce and Richard Reed Parry also became fast lifelong friends.

street.* A regular fixture in their social circle, Sufjan became a frequent sounding board for the Dessners during this period.

They also had their trusted producer, Peter Katis, who would play a bigger role than ever, so long as they could afford it. Thanks to "Secret Meeting" being placed in a Saturn car commercial the band had a little extra money to burn alongside the advance Beggars gave them, and they knew they were going to need it.[1]

> **Peter Katis:** They had a budget, but they were still really nervous about having enough time. By then they'd become my friends, so I said, "Okay, I'll give you a deal. You have enough money by my standards to pay for two months. I'll give you *three* months." That's a lot of time to make a record, but apparently it's not that much time for The National.

Scheduling their studio time for the summer, they spent that spring trying to write new material, but the songs weren't exactly coming to them easily.

> **Aaron:** Every time you start writing songs again, it's like starting from scratch. No matter how many good songs you write, it's as though you've never written a good one.

---

*Between *Alligator* and *Boxer*, Bryce also played in Sufjan's band alongside violinist Marla Hansen, who would ultimately sing on *Boxer*, and horn players Ben Lanz and Kyle Resnick, who became permanent staples of The National's live band on the *Boxer* tour.

Bryan: On *Alligator* we had most of the songs ready, at least conceptually. On *Boxer*, it felt like we didn't have any songs at the beginning. There was much more agony trying to get stuff going.

By this point, a National song would generally begin like this: first Aaron or Bryce would write the skeleton of a song on their own as a simple guitar pattern or, for the first time ever, a piano line. From there it would be composed as a multi-track demo using a bedroom Pro Tools setup.

Aaron: With *Boxer* there started to be a lot more intent. I was definitely trying to lean into ideas that I thought would really click for Matt lyrically and melodically. I knew this pocket or tempo that might click best for Bryan, or a way of playing might really spark with Bryce.

Bryce: I think we were still really trying to push the envelope of what a song could be, searching for the most original, least referential sounds. It was like we were rejecting anything familiar until we could come back to it through some unexpected doorway.

Once the demo was made, the band might convene to develop things further, while Matt began fiddling with lyrics and melodies. Not everyone was impressed with the sketches at first.

Aaron: When we first got together to rehearse, Bryan told me it all sounded like elevator music, which kind of hurt.

Bryan: That sounds like something I would say.

Boxer began with a pool of around 20 such sketches and demos, which the Dessners would give humorously random placeholder titles. Some tunes—like the surf rocky "Body Mailer," the U2-sounding "Grapes," and the Sonic Youth-flavored "O'Rourke"—would be aborted somewhere along the way. Others—like the Television-tinged "Marquee Moon" ("Guest Room") and the Pixies-inspired "Pixies" ("Mistaken for Strangers")—were semi recognizable embryos of the songs that would eventually end up on the album.*

A good example of how things sounded at this juncture is the "Slow Show" demo, found on the 2008 B-sides compilation *The Virginia EP*, where sparsely layered guitar, banjo, and toms delicately prop up Matt's nonsensical mumbling. While these starter tracks contained the foundations the songs would be built upon, they remained hugely unfinished heading into the studio.

> **Carin:** There is something to be said for when everyone's ambitions outstrip their confidence. You have to force yourself into it, because you haven't done it yet. That's such an exciting, fertile place.

* * *

---

*"Gospel" is a rare example where Matt kept Aaron's original title.

8
Apartment Story

Not long before work on *Boxer* began, Matt and Carin decided to move in together.

> **Carin:** We had been dating for a while.
>
> **Matt:** We had split up once or twice earlier in our relationship, but by this time Carin and I were pretty sure that we were gonna stay together.
>
> **Carin:** We used to just stay at each other's apartments and argue over why there was no reason to combine apartments until there was. He was going on tour a lot, so we were like, *Should he still be paying rent?*
>
> **Matt:** I had never lived with anyone romantically. There was a lot of anxiety about jumping into that.
>
> **Carin:** We're both natural worriers.

The domicile in question, which Carin had originally occupied with her sister, was a two bedroom unit on the top floor of a handsome brownstone in picturesque Clinton Hill, Brooklyn. It was one of those rare deals New Yorkers dream of.

Carin: It was this magical spot because it was really big,
but they weren't trying to get top dollar for it, so it
was much nicer than we should've been able to afford
at that stage.

Unwilling to fill up the place with the crappy furniture they
could afford, they kept the spacious living room open, with
the exception of two peach-colored armchairs that Matt
had spotted at a vintage store and turned out to be painfully
uncomfortable to sit in. Furnished or not, the apartment
incubated a potent songwriting partnership that continues
to this day.

Matt: Carin has a couple of lines on *Alligator*, but *Boxer*
is the record where she was really listening, giving
feedback, and writing bits and pieces all the time

Just like the rest of the band had established a process for
writing the music, Matt had a scheme for crafting lyrics,
which took over the entire apartment. At any given hour
you could find him writing lyrics by hand in various rooms
and corners, often bent in strange positions like an antenna
trying to pick up a signal.

Matt: It was a process of just writing down every thought
I had. I always had a notebook, all over my house and
everywhere I was going.

Carin: They were these big, thick notebooks that he
would fill with lines, which he organizes with this
internal system of colored underlines and dots. Then
he would start filling new notebooks with the pickings

and start arranging them around songs. He has the whole blueprint in his mind.

Taking on her natural role of editor, Carin would critique Matt's work whenever he asked.

> **Matt:** She's a great editor. She'd say, "This feels disingenuous," or tell me when I'm circling the same thing too much, like, "You're stuck in that one image." She would push me or give me permission to go into new directions.

Other times she would write together with him, or separately beside him. And when he wasn't looking she would add her own words and underlines on top of his.

> **Carin:** I would write in the notebooks when he wasn't there, and if some of my lines didn't make it through the transition from one notebook to another, I would just add them back in so they didn't get forgotten.
>
> **Matt:** She filled in a lot of gaps and provided a lot of indelible, unforgettable images.

As Aaron and Bryce shared sketches of the music, Matt would start assigning lyrics to the ones that resonated and playing with melodies, a state of limbo known as the "mumbling phase." While the words would add layers of feeling to the seedling songs, the emotional core was already there.

> **Matt:** Aaron writes music that's really emotional. His palette has a poignancy and a melancholy already in it. I write a lot about those things too, but the core sketch of Aaron's music is the water that I jump into.

Carin: The music was so stirring and layered, in ways
that managed to be both grandiose and cutting and
depressing. There was that decaying elegance to it. We
knew the lyrics and the performance had to compete.
There was a sense of approaching the record as a whole.

In the hunt for a common vision and style, Carin and Matt
would have long philosophical discussions about voice, themes,
characters, and how words and music enhance each other.

Carin: The idea was to sit inside what the music is already
doing to create another resonance. It's like when letters
have colors; certain words in the context of certain
instruments took on a paintinglike image in your head.

When the pair wasn't writing, they were reading, with Carin's
weighty bookshelf of modern and contemporary literature
functioning as inspirational textbooks for Matt's wordplay.

Matt: She started lending me a lot of her books, helping
me chew on words in a different way through poets
like John Ashbery and Robert Lowell, and writers like
Grace Paley and Joan Didion.

Carin: There was a lot of John Berryman being read at
the time. I'm always reading a lot of Louise Glück.
Matt was reading a lot of Jonathan Ames.

Matt: I stole that line in "Guest Room" about throwing
money at each other and crying from Grace Paley.
"Showered and blue blazered" on "Mistaken for
Strangers" is from the Jonathan Ames novel, *Wake Up,
Sir!*

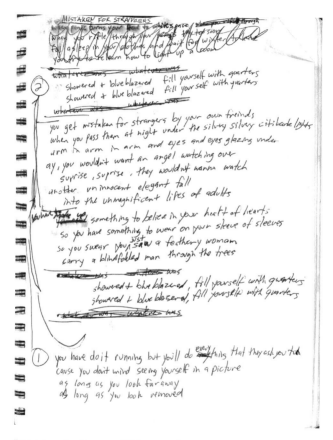

"Mistaken for Strangers" (Courtesy Matt Berninger)

One particular work of fiction by John Cheever left an especially lasting impression on Matt and the character he was developing on *Boxer*.

> **Matt:** I was really in a big Cheever phase, and I was just obsessed with "The Swimmer."

A classic allegory on aging and suburban isolation, the 1964 short story in question follows an upper class drunk who decides to travel home by swimming across his neighborhood's manufactured waterway of backyard pools. Along his quixotic journey he encounters increasingly estranged acquaintances—as day turns to night, summer shifts to autumn, and his youthful vigor fades—only to find his house empty and abandoned at the end.[1]

> **Matt:** It's depressing and beautiful and funny. I remember that story resonating with me so much. *Boxer* was very much inspired by that dreamy, delusional, slightly-inebriated midlife phase that Cheever wrote about so well.

As their budding songwriting partnership began to blossom, their creative chemistry was obvious: the spotlight-loving frontman now had a critical eye to purify his endlessly flowing poetry, and the bookish editor had an eager surrogate to act out the memorable character she was helping bring to life.

> **Matt:** *Boxer* was the one where Carin was really raising the bar for me. She wasn't letting me be lazy about the

writing, and I was dragging her into it with me. I was trying to impress her more than anybody.

Carin: What was so fun about it was that he was such a good performer. I saw the character that he was doing, and it was fun to try to write for that guy. I couldn't resist thinking, *What does it sound like if he talks about this?*

In the same way that their shared idol Tom Waits began doing his most adventurous work when he began collaborating with his wife Kathleen Brennan, Matt's best work began with Carin.

Matt: I remember feeling so good about the lyrics. I didn't have much confidence in my voice, but I felt I was becoming a good writer. Carin gave me so much confidence as a writer. It's been like that on every record since.

*   *   *

9
Bob Dylan Shat in My Room

In late June, The National arrived at their home-away-from-home, Tarquin Studios, where they would spend much of the next three months trying to bring *Boxer* to life.

Bryan: Tarquin Studios is the ultimate bubble world, because you don't have to leave. It's this massive old Victorian house with three floors and six bedrooms. There's this whole rhythm to life there.

Scott: It's sort of the perfect scenario if you're going there to work. We spent a lot of time over the years just living in Peter's house with him, which is kind of weird but part of the deal. I don't know if any bands stayed as long as we did.

Big enough to get lost inside its cavernous confines, and just far enough away from the distractions of New York, the house fostered an animated summer camp atmosphere, which was fun for the people who didn't already reside there.

Peter Katis: My wife and I used to live in the house, and that's certainly part of the story of *Boxer*. It was insanely overwhelming over the course of that summer, and a little bit traumatic.

While daily life revolved around the third floor recording studio, living quarters and the huge commercial kitchen were situated on the first two levels of the house. It was a brutally hot summer, so during the first weeks you could spot the band watching the 2006 World Cup in front of the living

The Dessners watching the World Cup. (Credit: Peter Katis)

room air conditioner. At night the crew would assemble in the galley for group meals.

Bryan: Dinner was always a big production.

Scott: We would go to Stop & Shop and get a bunch of groceries and stock the kitchen. Once a week Peter would make this insanely spicy chili that would destroy you. He basically lived on soup and Powerade.

On top of the band living, sleeping, and working there around the clock, the house was swarming with day-trippers, including engineering assistant Greg Giorgio, studio interns, friends of the band, and visiting musicians.

Peter Katis: With all the people and foodmaking it was just unrelenting. I had these big recycling bins that they would fill up in less than a day. I'd say, "You guys are bad for the earth!"

Peter's two cats were a mostly popular presence.

Bryan: One cat was named Petey and the other one was Bob Dylan. If you didn't shut your bedroom door, a cat would take a shit on your bed. One day I left my door ajar, and then I hear from upstairs, "All right, who just fucked up?" Bob Dylan shat in my room.

*   *   *

If the house were a human head, the studio would be its brain. Walking up the creaky steps from the kitchen, past

Bryan, Bob Dylan, and Bryce. (Credit: Peter Katis)

the second floor bedrooms, you would emerge into Peter's command center: the control room, where stacks of digital and analog gear, a roving computer monitor, and speakers of all sizes surrounded a ten-foot mixing console. Through an oversized rectangular window, you could peer into the spacious "live room" where much of the recording was done.

Behind Peter's thronelike swivel chair was a wide green sofa where spectators would gather. Beneath vaulted ceilings, the low-hanging corners of the room were lined with rows of guitars and keyboards, while drums, amps, mic stands, and coiled-up cables lived in the other room.

While Peter refereed this field of music-making dreams, The National called the plays. As usual, Aaron and Bryce were determined to milk as much precious studio time as they could out of the summer.

Scott: We'd stay up there for days at a time, usually five days a week. Peter tended to work pretty late, but there was a cutoff.

Bryce: When Peter got married, he stopped working weekends, which was a huge blow because we were used to 12-hour days nonstop.

Peter Katis: If you weren't sleeping, you were working. I would show up to unlock the studio in the morning, and the Dessner brothers would be standing there by the door.

Bryce: We were just relentlessly pushing. I think we drove him a little crazy.

To smooth out the intensity of their mission, alcohol played its own part in the process.

Aaron: We drank a lot.

Matt: Everybody was stressed out.

Aaron: We would start making drinks to blow off steam, so the days got less productive as they went on.

Peter Katis: No one was shy about getting loaded. Matt had chosen to drink whiskey out of a huge beer mug. They were not allowed to get anywhere near the computer in those days.

Scott: Peter wouldn't drink until he was done for the
night. He was pretty strict about his process.

Aaron: We'd try to get him to drink and mix by chanting,
"Drink and mix! Drink and mix!," but he wouldn't do it.

Peter Katis: When I'm working, I have no interest in
having a drink at all. There's just too much to screw
up.

With the twins intent on making a heavily orchestrated
record, Padma was around more than ever, recording violin
and viola takes, and composing sweeping string and horn
arrangements around their in-progress tracks.

Bryce: Padma's contributions were really wild and beautiful
for songs like "Ada" and "Mistaken for Strangers."
"Gospel" has this beautiful slow-moving vocal
arrangement. You'd be hard pressed to find something
like "Squalor Victoria" on other rock records.

Boxer also marks the first time the band worked with pianist
Thomas Bartlett, best known then by his recording project
Doveman, who would go on to play on every National record
thereafter.*

Peter Katis: Thomas is an amazingly talented guy. He has
this very specific skill where he can re-voice chords in
a way that makes the song so much more emotional
or sad.

---

*Little did The National know that, on top of being a gifted musician,
Thomas was also moonlighting as a music columnist for Salon.com, where
he ranked *Cherry Tree* his number 1 album of 2004.

Thomas's premier contribution, which found him doubled up with Bryce on piano, would turn out to be the first thing you hear when you drop the needle on *Boxer*.

Thomas Bartlett: I drove up from New York in my little hatchback filled to the brim with keyboards. As I'm still unloading things into Peter's studio, Bryce says, "I wrote this song. It's probably not going to be on record, but there's this piano part that's difficult to play, so we've been recording it one hand at a time. Can you play the two parts together?"

Padma and Thomas facing off in the studio. (Credit: Peter Katis)

That song was, of course, "Fake Empire."

*   *   *

With huge aspirations, months of possibility, and a healthy dose of not knowing what the record should sound like, Tarquin Studios became a laboratory of sonic experimentation. Everyone was in full mad scientist mode.

> **Matt:** On *Boxer* we realized, if we're gonna last, we can't phone this in. We were looking in every drawer and pulling on every string, combining things that you can't possibly make work together.
>
> **Bryce:** We were experimenting a ton, and searching deeper. Whereas *Alligator* was a rock record with some interesting orchestration from Padma, we were turning over every stone with sonic experiments, playing with whatever we could get our hands on.

When they weren't adding classical flourishes and atypical time signatures, they were abusing their instruments to create abrasive textures and scouring the rest of the house for unusual sound sources.

> **Aaron:** For a while we had this whole other two minute outro for "Brainy" that was based on the sound of the oven fan in Peter's kitchen because we thought it sounded cool.

With only so much that could be recorded upstairs at once, it became evident that they needed multiple tracking scenarios. So with the help of Brandon Reid they set up a secondary recording space in an unfinished basement storage room. Pushing aside boxes, bed frames, and Peter's malodorous hockey equipment, they hooked an old blue Power Mac to a portable mixing console and dubbed this makeshift Studio B "Bongo Island," which they christened by taping up a childlike drawing of a desert island and palm tree on the door.

Scott: I think Bryan named it. Or did Peter?

Bryan: It was probably Scott, Peter, or me. Maybe Brandon?

Brandon Reid: I'm 80 percent sure Bryan coined "Bongo Island."

Peter Katis: It definitely sounds like Bryan.

Bryan: There were no actual bongos.

A meticulously researched recreation of the Bongo Island sign. (Artist: Tana Pinkard)

Regardless of who gave it such an overly flattering name, the glorified closet became a centralized hub for weirdness.

Brandon Reid: We were able to fuck around without the pressure of being in the main studio, trying to record things that might sound cool in the mix.

Aaron: Bryan would get stoned and hit on pipes.

Brandon Reid: We would find items that were in the basement, he'd bang on them, and we'd record it.

Bryan: There was a broken fan encased in a wire cage that made this metallic rattle if you hit it. I think that ended up on "Apartment Story."

Scott: I recorded my guitar part for "Brainy" down there.

Brandon Reid: I played the floor tom on "Gospel."

While Bryan recorded the most in Bongo Island, Scott put in many an hour laying down potential bass and guitar lines.

Brandon Reid: Scott's a different creature in the studio. The Dessners are the type who deliberately write their parts, whereas Scott searches for his ideas through jamming.

Although beloved by all, the ultimate value of Bongo Island is still up for debate.

Peter Katis: Bongo Island is where overdubs went to die. They basically tracked in there every day, and we used virtually nothing from it.

Aaron: If you listen, you'll hear the Bongo Island parts here and there, especially at the ends of songs.

Brandon Reid: I don't think we were emotionally connected to anything we were doing down there.

With the house literally shaking all hot summer long, Peter's wife Ann was an innocent victim of The National's creative lunacy.

Peter Katis: It was ungodly how loud it was. There was the studio blasting, people making music in bedrooms, and then Bongo Island right below my wife's living room. Today she insists she has fond memories of that summer, but at one point she called me crying from downstairs, saying, "I can't take it anymore!" It was just so overwhelming.

*   *   *

More akin to Petey and Bob Dylan than the other guys in the band, Matt was an elusive presence at Tarquin. While others might be laying down endless takes upstairs or clanking on found objects, he was often self isolating in his room, hiding out in private nooks and crannies, or testing out vocals in Bongo Island at odd hours of the night.

Peter Katis: "The Dark Lord" became one of Matt's many nicknames because he was just sorta moping around, trying to write lyrics.

Matt: I'd do a lot of pacing outside with my notebook. The house had a nice porch and I would just be out there on my own, drinking a lot of wine, smoking a lot of cigarettes, writing a lot of words.

Bryan: There was a lot of smoking and pacing. Matt smoked Marlboro Lights with the white filter, while I smoked a brown filter. I remember there was this jam-packed ashtray with his white cigarette butts outnumbering mine five or ten to one.

Matt: I'd come up to the studio and people would pop their heads out like, *Does he have lyrics yet?* It's stressful for those guys waiting for me to write.

In tandem with the words themselves, Matt had to figure out how he would actually sing them. Using GarageBand for the

The Dark Lord. (Credit: Peter Katis)

first time, he was giving everyone a run for their money in terms of the sheer number of versions.

> **Matt:** I'll come up with 25 different melodies for a song, with just a lot of mumbling and free associating. A good melody is like flypaper; words just start to stick to it.

While the Dark Lord's cloistered ways estranged him from the band at times, it befitted his lonely and restless search for his best work yet.

> **Bryce:** This was the beginning of a period where Matt became very solitary and protective of his process. It wasn't an open door, *Come in and see what I'm doing,* kind of thing. He was very studied and methodical trying to find the right thing.

> **Matt:** Early on it became a thing where if I put in words that were just for placement, those guys would get so attached to them that it would be a battle trying to change anything. So then I stopped sharing half-baked stuff.

*   *   *

10
Eeyore on Nyquil

Amid the creative cacophony, tracks started to come together to varying degrees of completion. The first one they laid down was a never-released but not insignificant song that Bryce sketched out, titled "Middleman," which begins:

In your city you didn't make a sound
Broke your fishbowl and you fell down
Heard a woman say, "Stay down,
champion, stay down"

You got up, got in a car
Said I don't think I'm going to go very far
Just take me one time around the ballroom
Take me one time and take me home

Though the song was quickly abandoned because Aaron thought it sounded too much like Arcade Fire, those two stanzas were repurposed for the end of "Tall Saint," another discarded demo that appears on *The Virginia EP*. The command "Stay down, champion, stay down" would also prophesize the record's eventual pugilistic theme.

Another rejected tune, "Forever After Days," goes:

Forever after days
Stand and make myself a crown
To the table I step alone
Hold my own above the ground

Take my shot under the light
Heroes come the common way
Pull myself into the sky
Wrap me in the banner I made

With the line "stand and make myself a crown," the band submitted the track as a potential jingle for Crown Royal whiskey, which was a bold move given the rest of the lyrics' less than subtle masterbation references. (Just read it again.) Inconceivably, Crown Royal passed on the opportunity.

The first bona fide keeper was *Boxer's* lead single and indisputable rock standout, "Mistaken for Strangers." Juxtaposing some nasty guitar work and Bryan's pipe banging with a swelling arrangement of oboe, bassoon, and trombone from Padma, the track helped set a thematic formula for how other *Boxer* tracks would be constructed. It also gave birth to a classic piece of National studio lingo.

> **Peter Katis:** That's where I invented the term "C.B.A."
> We were trying every possible combination of
> muting and unmuting things in the pre-choruses.
> Scott recorded those clangy guitars in Bongo Island,
> which to me absolutely made the song. At one
> point Bryce goes, "Turn off Scott's guitar," and I was

Peter twisting knobs. (Courtesy Peter Katis)

like "WHAT?! That's the best thing there! Can't be argued." That card can really only be used once a record.

*   *   *

As the lyrics to the songs began taking form, some major motifs began emerging from Matt's notebooks.

Even though none of the songs on *Boxer* are explicitly topical, the smoldering political atmosphere of Bush's second term stained the songwriting on a spiritual level. If *Alligator* was the angsty overture of the 2004 election, *Boxer*

Fake Empire

~~brand new shiny promises~~
birds in my ~~sleeves~~
~~driving~~ ~~straight~~ to you

stay out super late tonight
picking apples making pies
put a little something in our lemonade and take it with us
were half-awake in fake empire   "   "

tip toe through our shiny city
with our diamond slippers on
~~do~~ our gay ballet on ice bluebirds on our shoulders
were half awake in a fake empire   "   "

~~lets not try to figure out~~
~~every single thing at once~~

turn the light out say goodnight
no thinking for a little while
lets not try to figure out
everything at once
its hard to keep track of you falling through the sky
were half awake in a fake empire   " " " "

"Fake Empire" (Courtesy Matt Berninger)

was the bruised follow-up, finding the once resilient Mr. November slumped over a barstool, watching scrolling TV news bulletins of . . . *Troop Surges in Afghanistan and Iraq . . . Torture at Guantanamo and Abu Ghraib . . . Thousands Dead or Missing After Hurricane Katrina . . .*

Matt: By *Boxer* we were a year or so into Bush's second term. It was like, *God, when is this going to be over?*

Carin: It was terrifying, the dailiness of it. For people our age, that presidency coincided with the world looking very different than it had been presented previously. There was a feeling of growing disgust with things.

In response to the doom and gloom all around them, Matt and Carin found themselves closing the blinds and seeking shelter from the storm, occasionally unlocking the door to take out empty wine bottles or cracking the window to let the cigarette smoke out. Songs like "Fake Empire" and "Gospel," and later "Apartment Story," are foremost escapist anthems about forging domestic bliss in a frightening world.

Carin: We talked a lot about how you write love songs with a sense of global disaster in them. We were picking that out of the music.

Matt: So many songs on *Boxer* are just about avoiding the scary stuff: being at home, putting Christmas lights out in the garden, drinking wine, and smoking cigarettes with somebody you love.

As lovely as this honeymoon period was, Matt was also reflecting on how moving in with someone can be a rude awakening to the inescapable bullshit of any relationship. This included the head games—*You keep changing your fancy, fancy mind every time I decide to let go* ("Brainy")—the maintenance—*Do you really think you can just put it in a safe behind a painting, lock it up and leave?* ("Start a War")—and the diplomacy—*Ada don't talk about reasons why you don't want to talk about reasons why you don't wanna talk* ("Ada").

> **Carin:** Matt likes to play around with the stuff that scares him. I think he was interested in what it is that's so scary about getting intimate with another person, and the ways your own romantic fantasies melt in the face of reality.
>
> **Matt:** When you're in a serious relationship, you're trying to figure out if this is who you're going to spend the rest of your life with, and so you put it to the test. Carin and I were not only in love, we were in the heat of trying to figure out if we were going to make it together.

Tied into this domestic scene, you also find our Cheeverian protagonist clashing with age and the unintended consequences of partnering up. On "Guest Room" he admits to feeling like a jerk for hiding away at home while missing the rambunctious days of yesteryear. On "Green Gloves" he reminisces about the pals he hasn't called who are probably out getting drunk without him. On "Mistaken for Strangers" he describes walking right past his own friends while locking arms with his love.

Matt: I was in my mid-30s reckoning with youth and innocence being behind me. You have these dreams that you're gonna find this meaning in life. I'd kind of found it, but I was still struggling with that feeling of *What am I missing out on?* No matter what happiness you achieve, it's still filled with holes. I'm always writing about that mental condition.

No line on *Boxer* sums up the tragically anticlimactic woes of comfortably aging as well as the "Mistaken for Strangers" refrain: "Another uninnocent, elegant fall into the unmagnificent lives of adults."

Resentful he was still freelancing graphic design gigs, and fearful he might have to return to office work, Matt couldn't help but ruminate on the workingman's blues of the urban professional on "Squalor Victoria" and "Racing Like a Pro," where he chides the pink, young middle-class man climbing up the corporate ladder for the price of his soul.

Matt: I loved my old job, but at the end of the day I was stressed out and working these long hours building a website that's supposed to sell neckties when all I wanted to do was make art.

Weaving together *Boxer's* interrelated subjects, Matt had come to master his trademark minimalist imagery. For example, his frequent use of color, clothing, and anatomy—*green gloves, blue blazers, blue ribbons, white shirts, diamond slippers, empty tuxedos,* and many *sleeves* and *arms*—are packed with potential meaning.

Carin: Matt's natural images of suits and clothes—things you cover and armor and entertain yourself with—have a way of reminding you of his own vulnerability. I think he was writing about recent feelings of: *How do you step into these suits of adulthood and feel like they fit right?*

Similarly, his carefully selected fragments of decaying Americana—*apple pies, cakes, punch tables, American dictionaries, magazines, televisions, and yards with cars, gardens, and pools*—suggest *Boxer's* midcentury suburban milieu without limiting it to one interpretation.

Matt: The writers that I always loved are the writers that don't fill in too many details. They don't spell out how they feel; they illustrate little blurry fragments that anybody can relate to and give a listener a place to walk around in and feel like they're in the scene of a movie.

Carin: He's so good at taking an object that we all know and, in a couple of words, giving it so much signifying context. They're stray details but they're loaded.

* * *

After being nearly obliterated on the ill-fated *Alligator* recordings, Peter and Bryan set out to record the drums on *Boxer* as perfectly as possible, at one point setting up fourteen mics at once, before scaling back to five.

Peter Katis: I love drums, and Bryan is one of my favorite drummers period, so I would always push to

have the drums loud. More than any other National
record, the drums on *Boxer* are allowed to play a huge
role.

Bryan: I'm always trying to make things sound super
thuddy, dry, and dead. There's something so elusive
and appealing about getting that perfect snare sound.

Revealing the instant payoff of good drum tracks, songs like
"Mistaken for Strangers," "Brainy," and "Squalor Victoria"
showcase some of Bryan's most signature parts, which leap
into the forefront as the lyrics' main sparring partner.

Matt: The drumming on so many of these songs defined
what our band was: this strange, precise pounding,
like an animal with a rigid metronome.

Bryan: The key to understanding what I do is
understanding the bands we're channeling: Joy
Division, The Cure, The Smiths, The Walkmen . . .
The beat on "Mistaken for Strangers" was me writing
out the beat to Interpol's "Take You On a Cruise"
and altering it. The beat in "Squalor Victoria" is
similar to New Order's "Age of Consent" but slowed
way down.

While Bryan will be the last man on the planet to give himself
credit for originality, his thundering work on *Boxer* would
signal his arrival as one of the great drummers in all of indie
rock.

Bryan: There are a billion boring drum parts recorded
already, so who needs another? I guess I'm trying to

Bryan searching for that perfect snare sound. (Credit: Peter Katis)

find something that not only feels good, but feels a little different.

*   *   *

Midway through the summer there was the realization that, with the exception of "Mistaken for Strangers," the album lacked any discernible rockers.

Aaron: The rock songs are the hardest to find.

While Aaron managed to sketch a rollicking new song that would ultimately become "Apartment Story," this effort was complicated by the fact that Matt had drawn a hard line in the sand: he would not be screaming on this record.

> **Matt:** I didn't want to scream my head off anymore. It's so aggro, and when it happens live, with me losing my shit onstage, I go to this crazy, unhinged place. I didn't want to calcify into that kind of a person, much less that kind of artist. I wasn't in that place in my soul.

While the group wanted to respect their singer's wishes, it felt like an enormous risk to cut out their biggest attraction.

> **Aaron:** I think a lot about setlists, and the most popular songs in our live shows at the time were "Mr. November," "Abel," "Murder Me Rachel," and "Available." That was a vital gear for us, so it was a big deal not to do it at all.
>
> **Bryce:** Aaron was really pushing for it. One thing I give Matt credit for in a big way was that he was completely against it, as a principle, from the get-go.
>
> **Aaron:** It was clear to him that he didn't want to scream, so it was clear to us that we had to find another way.

Although Matt's singing would become more skillful on subsequent albums, his lack of technique at this stage forced him to reach deep into his baritone and compensate with style.

> **Carin:** With Matt not screaming, he had to find all the other corners in his voice. One of the ways he would

do that is by singing in super different positions: laying on the floor, slouching in a chair, or putting the mic right up against his mouth.

As is only natural in a band of brothers, Matt's ever more melodramatic delivery became the fodder of some playful ridicule.

Bryan: This is probably when we started making fun of Matt more. Everybody in the band can do a Matt impression.

Matt: Listening back, I'm struck by how odd my vocals sound. Like, was I fighting for this sound? Because I sound a little like Eeyore on Nyquil.

*   *   *

While Aaron was a leading force for driving the studio work forward, his turbulent personal life occasionally bled into the recording process.

Aaron: My relationship was breaking apart in the middle of everything. There were moments where I was not doing so well, but everyone kind of helped me. Matt was a really good friend to me then, and obviously my brother.

Bryce: There were days that he disappeared from recording because of what was going on. For instance, I recorded all the Thomas Bartlett tracks

alone with Peter, which is always dangerous without
Aaron . . .

Thomas Bartlett: We were working on "Slow Show"
and I tried this little hook on the accordion. Matt was
really into it. The next day, when Aaron got back, they
were excitedly playing him what we had done, and I
could just see his face trying to not look upset.

Bryce: Aaron said something like, "This sucks. It sounds
like some folk band in an Italian village."

Thomas Bartlett: He was like, "Who are we, the
Counting Crows or something?" He was not pleased,
but eventually got overruled.

* * *

11
Circling the Vortex

As the summer dragged on, creative ambitions, endless experimentation, and daily drinking collided with reality, and it started to look like three months of straight recording wasn't such a hot idea.

> **Aaron:** We were still relatively inexperienced with recording. I don't think we realized that it's not possible to be productive recording 14 or 16 hours a day, day after day, week after week. I remember this weird, stale feeling of being hungover and having to start another day.

With so many different versions, the band became snowblind inside the storm of their own making.

> **Scott:** We had all these songs, but we were kind of struggling to create this nuanced result. We were throwing everything at the wall, with people working upstairs, and others downstairs in Bongo Island. It's hard to make something together as a group in that way.

It didn't help that, despite everyone being under the same roof, creative decisions were being made in subcommittees, only to be reversed later.

> **Peter Katis:** It was this constant Marx Brothers routine, where two of the guys would be working with me for three hours to create a new part, and then two other guys would walk up and destroy it. Then Matt would come up and destroy everything.
>
> **Matt:** Trying to write records is like fishing. Sometimes you just pull boot after stick after old tire into the boat. Someone would get attached when it sounded like we finally caught a fish. Then I'd look at it and be like, *Nah, I don't want that fish,* and toss it back.
>
> **Bryan:** That's where "Circling the Vortex" originated in our studio language. When you get to take 75, it's like, "Guys, I think we're circling the vortex . . ."

While The National is frequently called a democracy, it might be best likened to the United Nations, where resolutions require an absolute majority to pass.

> **Peter Katis:** Trying to please every member of the band is like trying to pass through the eye of a needle. Everything is either *too fancy pants, too knuckle-dragger, too much like Coldplay or Radiohead or Arcade Fire.* They've got a reason to dislike almost everything in their music, so getting everyone to be happy was tough.

As is bound to happen with such obsessive passion, especially when you're blowing through your advance, differences of opinion would occasionally escalate into arguments.

> **Brandon Reid:** The majority of the creative friction inside the band is broadly the Dessners versus Matt, but more specifically Aaron versus Matt. It's not an oppositional or adversarial relationship; it's just two strong-willed individuals with strong creative opinions.

> **Matt:** There were some pretty tense shouting matches, with people being really angry a lot. We're always really excited about the songs, and we fight over what we like and what we've added. We get too attached and emotionally invested, and it causes a lot of big feelings.

> **Peter Katis:** It's kind of hard for me to comprehend how well people ultimately got along, considering how intense the emotions were, but no one was ever a dick to each other.

*   *   *

At the peak of the madness at Tarquin, the band was visited by Mathieu Saura—a.k.a. Vincent Moon—who was capturing footage for what would become his first full-length documentary, and *Boxer's* companion film, *A Skin, A Night.*[1] Containing grainy, impressionistic, fly-on-the-wall moments from the making of the album, the film is a moody if less than informational cinéma vérité of The National in the trenches of their own creative war.

Early on, a confessional-style interview with Aaron gives the most idyllic impression of the atmosphere.

It's a good thing to get us away from New York City, to be here all together. That's part of the collaboration, being in this house, back and forth, upstairs, downstairs. Matt's in his room writing lyrics all the time and finishing his melodies. There's a nice feel about it in that way. It does take us a while to find what we're looking for. It's like we're on a hunt.

Later on, a somewhat more acerbic Bryce admits the pitfalls of the record's tedious approach.

We've been working on it now since January or February, so it's about six months we've been working on the music at least, which is amazing. It's potentially a huge waste of money. It's very possible. We're almost archaic the way we're doing this. So many bands make it at home, and we have that technology, we could. The way we're working now, where we're all working...we kind of just decided we would do it this way. It's a gamble. It's a risk. It's not something we're used to. It can be alienating.

Behind the scenes, Saura was more disturbed with the band's studio process than the final cut suggests.

Alec Hanley Bemis: I was around while he was taping. I remember him talking about the album, saying, "This is a disaster! It's coming across horribly! It's going to be awful!" Just being around the dysfunction of the band, and how much they were fighting, he was thinking, *This can't possibly end well.*

While the film doesn't include footage of the band arguing, it ends on an ominous note, as a stressed out Bryce expresses even more uncertainty with their unfinished progress:

The film comes at a very interesting time for The National, because it's after we've found our audience, but at the same time we're making this record which is taking forever. We're very much in the middle of something, we don't know where we'll end up . . . Maybe the record will be the film, and that's all we'll have is this film. The record that never came out. It could be . . .

Bryce: I have a memory of that moment. Mathieu got frustrated, left the room, and smashed a window

Tarquin Studios as depicted in *A Skin, A Night*. (Credit: Vincent Moon)

with his fist, and was bleeding. He witnessed a super intense period of time for us.

*   *   *

As September drew near, and the wheels continued to fall off, it became clear that The National would not be delivering a finished album to Beggars Banquet that fall as the band had originally intended.

> **Peter Katis:** I think we had 20 songs but nothing was moving towards completion. They kept re-recording songs over and over, throwing them out, going onto

Bryan, Scott, Brandon, Aaron, and Matt watching Peter mix. (Credit: Peter Katis)

new songs, then going back to the old ones. It was a lot of spinning in circles and not getting anywhere closer to finished.

Bryce: Part of it was that there was *too much* material.

Matt: We knew the writing was good, and we knew the music was good, but I don't know how confident anybody was that the armature of this record was going to work together.

Aaron: I was going through the beginnings of separation and divorce, so I was kind of losing it.

Most serious of all, they'd already eaten through 70 percent of their budget with less than half a finished album to show for it.[2]

Scott: We were trying a lot of things, living up there, paying for people to participate, and we still had to budget for mixing and mastering. It all adds up.

With the band hopelessly stumbling around the ring, it was Peter who finally threw in the towel.

Peter Katis: At that point I felt things were really off the rails. I said, "I think you guys have to go finish these recordings somewhere else. Finish everything, come back, and we'll mix the shit out of it." Aaron was like, "Okay, I'll see you in two weeks!" I'm like, "No, no, no. I want you to *really* feel like you're done. Then come back."

*   *   *

12
Waiting for Winter to Leave

After three intense months in Connecticut, the band retreated to Brooklyn and splintered off to work on new material, play a few shows, and hibernate for the winter. Shortly after returning home, during a barbecue at Jess Dessner's house, Aaron filled Sufjan in on their frustrating progress.

> **Aaron:** I told him about how we were struggling, how hard it was, and how I didn't know if we were going to make a good record, and he was like, "Well, that probably means it's going to be really good," because friction is interesting.

Though the band had rightly earned a break, the Dessners kept moving forward.

> **Aaron:** I definitely have a strong drive to finish something. If I'm not working I'm almost depressed, so I just have to keep going.

Perhaps subconsciously inspired by the ongoing wars in the Middle East, the twins wrote four new songs named after branches of the military: "Army" become "Apartment Story," "Navy" became "Santa Clara," "Coast Guard" became "Racing Like a Pro," and "Air Force" became "You've Done It Again, Virginia."[1]

Whereas *Alligator* was largely recorded in Bryce's attic bedroom at Jess's house, much of *Boxer* ended up being captured in the attic of Aaron's place down the street. Like lo-fi miniatures of Tarquin Studios, both houses were 1890s Victorians with stained glass and squeaky wooden floors.

Aaron: We re-recorded half of the album in the attic. Everything that wasn't drums basically. We started to fuck around a lot in search of stuff. Matt was off writing more too.

Matt: I was just smoking cigarettes, drinking wine, reading a lot of Cheever, and talking to Carin about everything.

Bryce: Bryan was around to do percussion overdubs. I'm sure Scott came by.

Scott: We only really fully convened to work together at Peter's.

In an ironic reversal from the shoddy recordings that Peter had to salvage on their previous albums, Aaron and Bryce decided that these new songs were recorded *too well*.

Aaron: A lot of the guitars that we recorded at Peter's sounded too "studio" to our ears, so we went back and re-recorded all the guitars the way we had for *Alligator*. I think part of *Boxer's* charm is the hi-fi drums and the less hi-fi stuff going on around them.

> **Bryce:** We were engineering it ourselves with really shitty microphones. At the time my Pro Tools skills were better. Aaron's whole producer thing came later.

On top of scuffing things up, the attic phase was largely about problem-solving the many songs that just weren't quite jibing. In many cases it was about adding the minute but essential details that finally made the songs work, like Marla Hansen's gauzy backing vocals, Bryce's flute-fluttered intro on "Brainy," and Padma's crowning brass fanfare on "Fake Empire."

> **Bryce:** The way "Mistaken for Strangers" shifts to woodwinds at the end is really key for that whole song, but it was an epic search finding that detail. Now those kinds of moves are more natural for us, but at the time we were learning.

Upon *Boxer's* eventual release, the most eye-catching name to appear on the album's credits was unquestionably the Dessners' friend and neighbor, Sufjan Stevens. Although Sufjan was a good pal, he was also one of *Pitchfork's* most infallible stars—most recently with 2005's seminal *Illinois*—so asking him to help out on a National record was no small request.

> **Bryce:** I had been playing in his band, so I was the one to ask him. At the time it was kind of a big deal. We weren't on that level yet.

Graciously, Sufjan agreed, and over a single day they rented out a nearby basement studio, where he improvised piano parts for several cuts, effortlessly adding piano arpeggios to "Racing Like a Pro" and counter melodies to "Ada" and "You've Done It Again, Virginia."

Bryce: Creatively, Sufjan is the best studio musician I know. His contributions were of another world as far as injecting new musical energy into the band.

Aaron: He can run circles around pretty much anyone musically. I think we used the first take on "Ada." He just hears it and responds to it.*

* * *

As the Dessners were tracking overdubs down in Ditmas Park, Matt and Carin were fine-tuning words and melodies in Clinton Hill. To allow Matt to record new vocal takes, Brandon Reid drove up from Philly to jury rig a vocal booth inside their apartment.

Brandon Reid: We had a little tent enclosure in their living room, with a blanket tacked up to the ceiling that he would go inside of.

Carin: It was just a big microphone and a bunch of blankets in the middle of the room.

---

*As some form of reciprocation, Bryce and Aaron found time that winter to help Sufjan make one of his annual Christmas EPs, which they jammed out together in the attic. Years later it was officially released on the *Silver and Gold* box set, featuring album art by Jess Dessner.

Brandon ended up moving into their spare bedroom for a couple weeks to engineer. Working during business hours while Carin was at *The New Yorker*, the two laid down evolving takes for unfinished songs like "Slow Show" and "Apartment Story."

> **Brandon Reid:** We were drinking a lot of white wine. Matt would take long naps during the day. Then Carin would come home from work and review everything that we did with comments and corrections. Most nights we would work until 10 or 11 o'clock with her help.

> **Carin:** Matt thought it was very funny to watch me get up and try to get to work on time and never manage. I was staying up way too late trying to write songs, and then pretending it wasn't going to affect me during the day. I was tired all the time.

While "Slow Show," "Brainy," "Fake Empire," and "Gospel" are all somewhat about Matt and Carin, "Apartment Story," is most emblematic of their love story. While the song already had lyrics that the band was fond of, those cozy days spent indoors inspired Matt to rewrite it.

> **Bryce:** There was a big battle about "Apartment Story" because the lyrics changed. Matt and Carin were cocooned up, staying inside, and that song is really about them. It was this really beautiful period in their relationship.

Setting the scene of getting dressed up for a make-believe cocktail party for two, the tune is a tender ode to the simple

~~Anywy~~ Apartment Star

Be still for a secon while I try & try to pin your ~~corsage~~ flowers on

can you carry my drink I have everything else I'm getting tied
while I tie my tie ~~and~~ all by myself forgetting why
~~forgetting why and~~
~~Army All things of the believe~~
Are diving over the balcony

Tired & wired we ruin too easy
Sleep in our clothes and wait for winter to leave

Hold ourselve together with our arms around the stereo
while it sing to itself or whatever it does
~~while~~ it sings to itself at its long lost loves
forgetting why I'm forgetting why
~~of the~~ things we did believe
are diving over the balcony

Tired & wired we ruin too easy
sleep in our clothes and wait for winter to leave
but I'll be with you behind the couch when they come
~~on a different~~ day just like this one

we'll stay inside   our rosy minded fuzz

~~we're in for it~~ ~~things will go well~~
~~so worry not~~
~~all thing are well~~
we'll be alright   we have our looks
~~bllr~~ ~~things of~~
~~they~~ perfume on
~~and~~

bbllly the stuff that we believe
is diving over the balcony

"Apartment Story" (Courtesy Matt Berninger).

routine of getting drunk ("I'm getting tied"), escaping inside the television set ("do whatever the TV tells us"), and finding communion in music ("hold ourselves together with our arms around the stereo") whilst hiding from the world ("we'll stay inside til somebody finds us") and weathering the season of literal and political darkness ("sleep in our clothes and wait for winter to leave").

> **Carin:** He was capturing that experience: the do-nothingness of initial coupledome in a city that's freezing cold.
>
> **Matt:** We just watched TV and drank wine and listened to music and smoked cigarettes. It seems disgusting now but we loved it.

Although Carin doesn't claim a writing credit on this song, she can be heard literally singing backing vocals on the chorus. She also gets credit for talking Matt into the perfect title.

> **Carin:** We had a terrible title for that one, and I remember convincing him to change it to "Apartment Story." He finds it unnecessarily complicated to give it a cutesy title if it's not a line in the song, but I felt like that one just wanted a net to collect everything in.

*　　*　　*

13
Stay Down, Champion, Stay Down

A week or two after New Year's Day 2007, in the dead of the cruel New England winter, The National returned to Tarquin Studios to knock out *Boxer* once and for all. After nearly a year of fighting, the toughest round remained.

Bryce: Mixing is always the most intense.

Scott: Making our songs work is often an excavation process. We're layering all this stuff up and then it becomes this morass you have to strip away.

With the record already delayed once, and Beggars eager to get the album into their spring release calendar, pressure was building on the label side.

Roger Trust: There was major stress. I'm sure the band was feeling it, and rightly so. I had it heaped upon myself.

Matt: That anxiety of finishing the record and getting it perfect was definitely hanging over us.

Aaron: That's when it got pretty dark.

The problem wasn't that The National couldn't have turned in a completed album earlier. It was that they refused to consider anything complete.

> **Peter Katis:** They'd basically finished the record, but instead of it taking two weeks, it took six weeks to mix. They moved the deadline back multiple times until the date it *had* to be done, just because they were constantly reinventing and redoing.
>
> **Scott:** We're always challenged by trying to push the creative process to the very last minute. We're always tweaking it.
>
> **Bryan:** When you're neck deep in it, endless revisions don't seem as counterproductive as they can be.

Whether they liked it or not, money was running out and deadline day was looming. As the band clashed over how to finish the album to everyone's satisfaction, a handful of tracks posed most of the problems.

> **Aaron:** A lot of the core ideas were there, but we were trying to figure out how to turn them into great songs without destroying them.
>
> **Bryce:** There were big arguments going on around finishing "Apartment Story," "Slow Show," and "Squalor Victoria." "Ada" was just impossible to figure out.
>
> **Peter Katis:** "Brainy" got reworked in so many ways that I sometimes forget how it actually ended up. There are so many versions it's depressing. I have 98 saved sessions of that song.

It was at this stage in the process, when ultimate decisions *had* to be made, that the "Shell Game," as the band calls it, really came into play.

> **Brandon Reid:** They negotiate with each other when they're finishing a record, and it's funny because they think they're being discreet about it, but they're not. Aaron thinks that if he lets Matt keep a part Aaron doesn't like, it'll allow him to keep a part that Matt doesn't like, and vice versa.

While their argumentative style seldom resulted in bad blood, things definitely boiled over during the finishing of "Apartment Story," after Matt re-tracked his vocals with a more aggressive affect.

> **Aaron:** The song felt like it was already there, so I wouldn't stop mentioning how in love I was with the previous vocals. At some point Matt just lost his temper and screamed my head off. That was the first time we ever had a shouting match like that.
>
> **Matt:** There was one of those disagreements every hour, on every song. That must have been the piece of straw that made me lose my shit.
>
> **Aaron:** I was really sore for a while, but then we ended up using the version I wanted anyway because Carin or someone preferred it too.
>
> **Matt:** A lot of those conflicts were about people demanding respect for their processes and how we got to where we were going. Nobody likes to be pulled by a leash or told, *No, you're done.*

Despite the agony and conflict, Aaron and Matt also seemed to take the most perverse joy in it.

> **Aaron:** We were stressed because we knew the songs were good.
>
> **Matt:** The whole thing felt like an uphill journey, but I just remember enjoying every step up the hill and feeling, *Oh my god, this is going to be fucking awesome.* I like the hike.

*　　*　　*

Just as everyone was starting to feel really good about what they had made together, the final major blow The National had to suffer occurred just days before the record was supposed to be finished. After sending a rough mix of the album to Beggars Banquet the week before, Aaron received a phone call from Roger Trust.*

> **Aaron:** I remember they didn't respond for 10 days, and then Roger Trust finally told us the truth, which was that they were really disappointed with it. He was like, "Some people feel it's not what the band is capable of."
>
> **Roger Trust:** As an unwilling messenger, it's not an episode I'd care to reflect on.

---

*It should be noted that various people recall the exact timing of the call differently, with some remembering it happening after the record was completely finished.

In the eyes of some at the label, who were betting on The National to become the next Interpol, or at least expecting a couple of classic screamers like "Abel" and "Mr. November," *Boxer* was not the record they were hoping for.

> **Scott:** Beggars was expecting something more like *Alligator*, not these layered orchestrations with pianos and odd time signatures.
>
> **Peter Katis:** They weren't even sure it was "releasable." That was the word they used. I won't name names, but someone high up was not digging it . . .

After toiling for more than a year over what they believed could be their masterpiece, the label's lukewarm reaction was a serious gut punch.

> **Peter Katis:** Everyone was like, *What the* . . . and Aaron was like, "I knew I shouldn't have said anything!" But there was no putting the genie back in the bottle. I remember Matt was sitting on the couch, just brooding. All of a sudden, he pops up and goes, "Fuck it! We'll buy the record back and put it out ourselves if we have to!"
>
> **Aaron:** Matt was like, "We should leak it!"

While the notion of going back to write more rock songs was momentarily considered, all parties agreed it was time to put an end to this madness. With their confidence rattled, they got back to finishing the album with the few days they had left.

> **Matt:** People weren't sure how it was going to go down, but we stuck to our guns. It was a combination of confidence and exhaustion.

Roger Trust: At the end of the day, it would have been disastrous for the band and the label if the album had been delayed further or shelved, so we just cracked on with it and got the job done.

Aaron: Instead of depressing us, those kinds of moments always made us weirdly more determined and confident. We thrived on that kind of bunker mentality, and we knew the album was good.

*   *   *

While a rose by any other name smells just as sweet, a great album deserves a great title. After kicking around album titles for months, including one-word epithets like "Amplifier," "Movie," "Limousine," "Silvery," "Driver," "Runner," and the Cheever-inspired "Swimmer," the record remained nameless until the very end.

Carin: I remember hoping that they had a title that felt strong. There were just so many soft and lovely things in the music, it just felt right to have a title that was curt and hard. It was almost like we were trying to name the character in the songs.

Matt and Carin were on the phone, with him pacing around at Peter's and her sitting at her desk at *The New Yorker*, when the word *boxer* came out of Carin's mouth.

Carin: I saw the word, said it to him, and his instant response was "No." And I knew why: because of Simon & Garfunkel, and it's the name of underwear.

But there was just something about it. It was an early moment of confidence where I said, "Just try it." Once you said it, it felt right.

Especially given recent feedback, that powerful metaphor of the boxer—that weary prizefighter, desperately punching for his survival—seemed to perfectly characterize The National's many struggles, both on the record and their greater journey as a band.

Carin: After we had the title, we realized there were so many resonances.

Matt: Carin saw how hard we were all fighting to hold onto this fantasy of being a rock band.

Carin: It fit with that feeling of being in a fight, a battle, a war. There was a lot of war going on at the time.

Matt: It was partly directed at our peers and judges, especially in New York and the indie rock journalism world where you could so easily get destroyed.

Carin: Even that image on the cover kind of looks like a boxing ring. I'm sure that's why the word rang true for everybody. It was there: the man alone, against all odds.

*   *   *

As was the case with every National album until *Sleep Well Beast*, Scott designed the album art himself, with input from Matt.

Scott: We prided ourselves on being involved in every aspect of it. I remember sitting on Peter's couch with my laptop, saying, "How about this?"

When it came to the boxy design scheme and the bright yellow accent, a natural evolution from the lime green of *Alligator*, Scott planted a joke that pretty much nobody would get.

> **Scott:** It has a box on it for *Boxer,* and that iconic yellow border comes from *National Geographic.* I just thought that was funny: The *National* and *National* Geographic.

For a group that could barely agree on anything, Abbey Drucker's photo of the band performing at Peter and Ann's wedding was an easy and unanimous choice.

> **Peter Katis:** I almost feel like everyone thought it at the same time, like, *What if that was the cover?* Everyone wanted it to work.
>
> **Scott:** We saw it and were like, *Oh my God, this is awesome!* It's a beautiful picture, it had a really cool old school vibe that made sense with the music, and everyone was in it. It was literally us doing what we were doing at the time with all the people who were involved with us. It was kind of magical.
>
> **Peter Katis:** I know everyone in the photo: I'm right in front of Matt dancing with my sister-in-law. My wife is with her friend. To the right are my parents, my brother Tarquin, Bryan's wife Beth, my brother Tom, and my nephew Henry. To the left is my friend Dave Zamboni and Brian Rosenworcel from Guster.

While the black vignette Scott added serves the purpose of focusing the viewer's eye on the band, Abbey admits she was a little bummed to see the scope of her original composition lost. Viewed in full—in hindsight of all that happened up to that point, and all that was about to happen—the shot illustrates a tipping point in The National's story as well as any photo could.

> **Abbey Drucker:** In the raw photo, you see how minimal the whole room is. And then you have The National, who don't know what's going to happen in the next five years of their lives. That moment in time was the beginning of something massive for them.

Once the theme of the album had been settled upon, Scott made a few final adjustments to the artwork. Over a black and white photo of the band with Padma and Mathieu Saura in a French meadow, the album's inner sleeve features two opposing imperatives, one from the abandoned "Middleman"/"Tall Saint" lyrics, and another from "Ada."

STAY DOWN CHAMPION STAY DOWN
LET THEM ALL HAVE YOUR NECK

> **Carin:** That kind of defensive pose is one way to approach that sophomore effort, the one where everybody's watching to see if you're going to choke or not.
>
> **Matt:** It's a "fuck you" kind of surrender, like, *Go ahead, have my neck. Let them have it all, but don't let it destroy you.*

* * *

In spite of their label's disappointing first reaction, Peter and the band raced to finish the record, which of course meant changing as many things as they could. Ever afraid of sounding too paint-by-numbers, many of the final tweaks were the aural equivalent of paint splatter.

> **Peter Katis:** With a day or two to go, Aaron says, "It's too clean!" And they just started adding overdubs and noises to make it sound more fucked up.

In a rare moment of harmony between Aaron and Matt, one of the better known—and contested—stories from *Boxer* occurred on the final day in the studio, as they were finally adding Matt's vocals to "Squalor Victoria."*

> **Aaron:** "Squalor Victoria" was a song Bryce wrote the music to, Bryan added the drum beat, and Padma wrote this beautiful arrangement to it. We all thought it was a breakthrough of some kind, but Matt didn't have the words for a long time.
> **Bryce:** We liked the music so much that we just forced it to exist.
> **Aaron:** Peter had gotten really attached to the music. He was like, "Oh, this is going to be cool! There's an instrumental on a National record."
> **Peter Katis:** It sounded great.
> **Matt:** Then he got pissed when I sang on it.
> **Aaron:** He was like, "You just ruined the song!" But I defended Matt, like, "No, he just *made* the song!"

*The timing of this is also disputed.

Peter Katis: Their version is that I put the singing in the
song and said, "This sucks, you ruined it," but hold
on. Someone imported these random, scatty demo
session vocals. It's not what you hear in the song now.
So I was like, "What the fuck is this?"

Aaron: It was one of our great truces.

Peter Katis: I do regret saying something that harsh. It
just came out. The problem with The National is that I
start acting like I do around my brothers.

*   *   *

Choosing a final tracklist for *Boxer* was also saved for the end.
Of the dozen or so songs that were dropped at various points
in the process, "Santa Clara" and "You've Done It Again,
Virginia" were the last ones left on the cutting room floor.

Aaron: We really loved those songs, but they were just a
little derivative or middle of the road, whereas all of
the songs that made it on the album are undeniable.

From the get-go they knew "Mistaken for Strangers" had
to exist near the top. Thinking in vinyl terms, their second
most upbeat song, "Apartment Story," felt like a good way to
kick off Side 2. The prayerlike "Gospel" felt like the perfect
closer. While it's hard now to imagine the album starting off
any other way, the biggest late changeup was to place "Fake
Empire" on top.

Peter Katis: For the entire summer "Start a War" was
supposed to be the opener, and "Fake Empire" was

always going to be the closer. Then right at the end someone said, "What if that's the lead off track?" And it was like, *Whoa . . .*

Matt: "Fake Empire" became this big cinematic thing with the added fanfare. It was such an entrance! We had to start with it.

Aaron: I remember sitting and playing around with the sequence on the couch really late into the night before mastering. I think we fell asleep on the couch trying to listen to it. I think it's a perfect sequence.

Side 1

1. Fake Empire
2. Mistaken for Strangers
3. Brainy
4. Squalor Victoria
5. Green Gloves
6. Slow Show

Side 2

7. Apartment Story
8. Start a War
9. Guest Room
10. Racing Like a Pro
11. Ada
12. Gospel

It was a gray February morning when everyone packed up to drive down to New York for mastering, where the final mix is set in stone. Although *Boxer* was supposed to be handled by legendary engineer Greg Calbi, who mastered *Alligator* and every National album since, the band had delayed so many times that Calbi could no longer squeeze the record in, forcing them to switch to a lesser-known engineer named Fred Kevorkian.

Peter Katis: He did a great job but his studio was extremely small. It has this gloomy lounge straight out of a David Lynch movie, with a table and chairs and fluorescent meat locker lights. Everyone was so overworked, with greasy hair and scarves on, thinking, *The label hates it. We're fucked.*

In their frail, overworked state, it was not lost on the band that their mastering engineer had the same last name as the famous proponent of assisted suicide.

Scott: He was great. No complaints. We just thought, *Is this an ominous sign?* We made this record and now Dr. Death is going to master it.

*   *   *

Upon returning to Brooklyn, the band organized a listening party for their friends at Jess Dessner's, where Bryce and Scott were now living.

Bryce: It was in the second floor living room, in the middle of the day. We had friends over. Sufjan was there. We all piled onto the couch and listened to the master on Scott's stereo.

Scott: There were a lot of candles lit. It was moody for sure.

Bryan: It was really loud.

Bryce: The vibe was really awkward, definitely not celebratory.

Bryan: Afterwards it was silent.

Aaron: When it was over nobody had anything to say. It was Sufjan or Matt who said, "Well, that was awkward."

Bryce: Sufjan was like, "Don't ever make me do that again."

Matt: It was the worst. I don't know why anybody ever does that.

*   *   *

14
Let Them All Have Your Neck

Two-thousand seven was a landmark year in indie rock. It may have been the greatest year in indie rock. For the voracious music blog reader, every day was an opportunity to discover a new favorite album or artist from the endless conveyor belt of releases, like Animal Collective's *Strawberry Jam*, Arcade Fire's *Neon Bible*, Battles' *Mirrored*, Beirut's *The Flying Club Cup*, Burial's *Untrue*, Bon Iver's *For Emma, Forever Ago*, Explosions in the Sky's *All of a Sudden I Miss Everyone*, Feist's *The Reminder*, Iron & Wine's *The Shepherd's Dog*, Jens Lekman's *Night Falls Over Kortedala*, Kevin Drew's *Spirit If . . .*, LCD Soundsystem's *Sound of Silver*, Liars' *Liars*, M.I.A.'s *Kala*, Modest Mouse's *We Were Dead Before the Ship Even Sank*, of Montreal's *Hissing Fauna, Are You the Destroyer?*, Okkervil River's *The Stage Names*, Panda Bear's *Person Pitch*, Radiohead's *In Rainbows*, The Shins' *Wincing the Night Away*, Spoon's *Ga Ga Ga Ga Ga*, St. Vincent's *Marry Me*, The White Stripes' *Icky Thump*, Wilco's *Sky Blue Sky*, Yeasayer's *All Hour Cymbals*. It was incredible.

Beside the standalone merits of each of these albums, what made this period so enthralling was how completely different every record was from the last. United by the internet and rapidly expanding beyond the hip confines of Brooklyn, this loosely connected culture of independent artists and listeners represented a paradigm shift in modern music. Steeped in decades of music history made accessible by iTunes, file sharing, and CD burning, their common hunt for variety and originality was leading to the dissolution of "genre" as both a descriptor of sound and a single group you were allowed to belong to. "Indie" wasn't a sound or a delineation of label status, it was a mindset. In all these respects, *Boxer* fit right in. Looking back, it would seem that after years of half-victories, The National was finally in the right place at the right time.

* * *

After 13 months of work, *Boxer* was finally done. And while everyone loved the album they'd created together, they knew its fate rested on how other people liked it.

> **Matt:** Everybody was really nervous about it. I remember being stressed out on an artistic level, like, *Are we gonna stay relevant?* We were happy that we weren't mimicking any of our more successful peers. I think there was confidence in it as a bold kind of record.

As Beggars Banquet and the greater Beggars Group— comprising 4AD, Matador, XL Recordings, Young Turks, and the since dissolved Too Pure—began mounting a comprehensive album campaign for *Boxer*, there were a few lingering signs of mixed internal enthusiasm.

> **Aaron:** Matt and I did the press trip together. We went to London and I don't think they had *any* interviews scheduled for us, which was very odd. We had a beer with the press guy and he was like, "Well, there's a White Stripes album coming out . . .," basically telling us *Boxer* wasn't what people were going to be thinking about.

Regardless of expectations, the label's New York office—which included Head of Marketing Matt Harmon, Director of Publicity Sonya Kolowrat, and Product Manager Miwa Okumura—was doing everything in its powers to make *Boxer* a success.

> **Matt Harmon:** I think people had seen the possibility of those guys finding a route to commercial radio, and there might've been a feeling of disappointment realizing that didn't actually exist.
>
> **Sonya Kolowrat:** When we started servicing *Boxer* to press, I was nervous about it, because I loved *Alligator*, and when you listened to *Boxer* for the first time it was like, *Where are screamers? Where's "Mr. November?"* Then you listened three more times and you were like, *Oh . . .* It just took a minute.
>
> **Miwa Okumura:** Everybody working on the album at the label felt personally invested. This was an opportunity for us to work an American band for a U.K. label that wasn't known for that. We really felt

ownership, like, *We want to make this work as much as you do.*

Never ones to sit idly by, the band was actively involved in strategy, and ready to jump at every opportunity.

Matt Harmon: As opposed to some of our other big bands, they would hang out. Aaron would come by the office to get lunch. Scott would come in to work on artwork. It was a familial feeling.

Having fully realized the competitive nature of the indie landscape after the Clap Your Hands Say Yeah episode, they were also carefully studying their peers.

Press Photo (Credit: Sonya Kolowrat)

Matt Harmon: Aaron would sit at my desk and we'd look at SoundScan together and see how bands like LCD Soundsystem were doing. It created competition in their minds.

While the label's promo strategy was to go as wide as possible, they knew their most important move was to solidify their existing base: namely the *Pitchfork*-reading hipsters of New York. On the final day of February, they were able to get *Pitchfork* to announce the album and its May 22 release date to the world with the snazzy headline: "Exclusive: The National Enter the Ring With *Boxer*."[1]

For folks at the label who were still anxious about what the press reaction would be, some nerves were calmed after sending the first batch of promos to select critics.

Stephen M. Deusner: I remember getting the heavily watermarked promo CD and being very specifically excited to write about it. It felt like kind of a big deal.
Sonya Kolowrat: I definitely got some phone calls saying, "Oh my God, this is amazing!" That's when I was able to report back and assure everybody, "Don't worry, we're good."

In middle March, their pal Mathieu Saura and *La Blogothèque* dropped a gorgeous Take Away Show of the band performing "Start a War" and "Ada" in France.[2] Beggars also made the decision to drop "Fake Empire" as a free mp3 download, giving people their first real taste of the album before officially releasing "Mistaken for Strangers" as a single in April."[3]

Matt Harmon: That song was just meant to set the mood. "Fake Empire" felt like a good way to move people off the rockers of the last record and get them ready for the more mature songwriting that was coming.

Then on March 31, as was inevitable in those days, *Boxer* leaked onto the internet seven weeks before its release date.[4] Whether the leak helped build hype for the album is a matter of speculation, but things definitely started snowballing over the next several weeks. By April 3, *Stereogum* had posted a glowing "Premature Evaluation" of the full album that ended with: "Could it be one of our favorites of the year? Yes, definitely."[5]

The next day Brandon Stosuy interviewed Bryan, Scott, and Matt for his *Stereogum* column "Quit Your Day Job," where they all expressed skepticism that they'd ever be able to stop freelancing.[6] Released shortly thereafter, the low-budget music video for "Mistaken for Strangers" is all the evidence you need that Beggars and the band weren't counting on a quick recoup of their advance.[7]

Playing into the label's strategy, nowhere was anticipation building more than on the streets of New York. Heading into May, The National had lined up a dramatic tour kickoff in their adopted hometown, beginning with three shows supporting Arcade Fire at Harlem's ornate United Palace and culminating with five consecutive headlining gigs at the revered Bowery Ballroom. All eight shows sold out more than a month in advance, after which a writer at *Brooklyn Vegan* pondered, "Can someone tell me how The National suddenly became the biggest band in the world?"[8]

* * *

When *Boxer* hit record stores, the reviews started pouring in. *Rolling Stone's* Rob Sheffield gave it four stars while shouting out Bryan's drumming and Matt's lonesome, warm baritone.[9] *The New York Times'* Jon Pareles honed in on the magical interplay between "verbal nuggets" and the "music's sheer intricacy."[10] While negative reviews were mostly nonexistent, publications like *Paste Magazine* labeled it a less thrilling sequel to *Alligator*,[11] while *The Guardian* called it "claustrophobic, minor-key U2-on-a-budget" music.[12]

At a moment when, for better or worse, an indie band's standing was largely decided by *Pitchfork*, no review carried as much weight as Stephen M. Deusner's longform assessment of *Boxer*.

> **Bryan:** I remember being on pins and needles wondering, *What's Pitchfork going to give us? What's the number going to be?*

Even more consequential than his strong, if not earth shattering, 8.6 out of 10 rating was the fact that it bore the site's coveted "Best New Music" distinction, which could almost single handedly guarantee an album's success in the indie sphere.[13]

> **Stephen M. Deusner:** I was really happy that my editor let me go there and give them Best New Music. I remember a lot of *Pitchfork* writers reacting to it.

Recognizing it as a more restrained work than its predecessor, Deusner carefully noted how *Boxer* requires "space and time to reveal its dark, asymmetrical passageways."

> **Stephen M. Deusner:** I kept going back to the idea of the album and the band as a grower. You have to spend some time getting used to this voice and this very skewed imagery. There was a pleasure being disoriented by it, and having to dig deeper and decipher.

He went on to focus on the drumming, theorizing that the album title could be a reference to how Bryan's "rhythms casually spar with Berninger's vocal melodies, jabbing and swinging at the singer's empathies and emotions."

> **Stephen M. Deusner:** He's putting the beat or the hit where you don't necessarily expect it, and in that way it becomes a lead instrument. It's keeping time, but it's also commenting on what's going on.

And he gave ample credit to Matt's fully-realized songwriting.

> **Stephen M. Deusner:** *Boxer* is where they sort of cordoned off a territory lyrically. That album has such a vivid sense of place and time and character and milieu. It's almost like the beginning of this larger story of him going into adulthood.

Circling back on *Boxer's* "grower" nature, Deusner finished his assessment by saying: "It's the rare album that gives back whatever you put into it."

Stephen M. Deusner: It's an album that absorbs your own experience and gives the listener room to create their own interpretations and find their own connections with it. It's not precious about what it means to say. It's very open to being heard and interpreted in different ways. And as *I've* matured, it's opened up for me in interesting new ways.

For the reasons Deusner describes, critical adoration for *Boxer* would continue to grow as it worked its way deeper into listeners' psyches. For the band, the measured but undeniable praise they got at the time was validation enough of their gruesome perfectionist struggle.

Bryce: Getting shit on by critics was par for the course. It was very expected. The fact that *Pitchfork* really liked *Boxer* meant a lot at the time.

*　*　*

Scheduled around the first 10 days of release, The National kicked off the *Boxer* tour with a rapid-fire series of gigs on both sides of the Atlantic, sandwiched between a huge stop a the 2,000-seat London Astoria and their five-night victory lap at the Bowery Ballroom, which has come to be referred to as the "Colonel Sanders run" because of the starchy white shirt and tie combo Matt chose to wear.* It was the triumphant moment they had longed for.

*Appropriately, Thomas Bartlett (as Doveman) opened one of the nights, as did Peter Katis' band The Philistines Jr—with Bryan filling in on drums.

Bryce: It was a real night and day shift properly selling out bigger venues on our own. Five Bowery Ballrooms was well beyond anything we had done before.

Aaron: Together with all the *Alligator* songs, we started to have a repertoire. That was a powerful thing at that time.

Brandon Reid: *Boxer*'s initial response live, with most of the shows selling out, very quickly turned the Clap Your Hands situation into something worth laughing about.

Then, as the sales numbers started rolling in, the good news kept coming. In its first week, *Boxer* sold just shy of 10,000

Packing the London Astoria. (Credit: Mauricio Carey)

copies, leading it to debut at #68 on the Billboard 200.[14] By week two it had eclipsed *Alligator's* two-year sales total.

> **Aaron:** On release week, Dawn Barger called me with some shocking number of pre-orders and sales. Something caught fire really quickly. It totally outperformed early on, and then it accelerated.

While there was no about-face from Beggars, any original skeptics there had been converted by *Boxer's* artistic brilliance and unconventional commercial appeal.

> **Bryce:** The label was definitely surprised by how well received the record was. We never had a big falling out over it, but it was the only time in our band's history we got that kind of feedback from them.
>
> **Roger Trust:** I'm sure there were many people who loved the album from day one, and others that grew into it after a period of time. It was a relative slow-burner, but just kept on selling and selling. Tens of thousands every month.

One surprise for everyone was how one track seemed to resonate the most with listeners. Somehow, nobody saw The National's most signature song coming.

> **Bryce:** We never thought that "Fake Empire" would be the biggest song we've written. The label didn't and the band didn't.
>
> **Miwa Okumura:** There was a show where they played "Fake Empire" and we just looked around and were like, *Fuck, that song is so anthemic.* We didn't realize

how much more reaction it would get than the singles.

As the summer heated up, The National was continuing to sell out every show while soaking in steady media coverage. In mid-July they made their network television debut on the *Late Show with David Letterman*, where they performed a glistening rendition of "Fake Empire," complete with a three-piece horn section and Thomas Bartlett on piano. In an odd moment of symbolism, Letterman came out at the end holding the Vince Lombardi Trophy, borrowed from NFL coach Tony Dungy, for Matt to cautiously reach out and touch.[15]

> **Matt:** When the record came out, it was like we weren't going to be forgotten about; this wasn't the end of us. With *Alligator* it was sort of like, *Okay, now we're on the ladder, and we just have to fight our way up it*. With *Boxer* it felt like we had crossed over into something.

With the album well on its way to paying for itself, Beggars ponied up the money for another music video. Whereas the "Mistaken for Strangers" video was filmed inside Matt and Carin's apartment with what looks like a handheld camcorder, the slick video for "Apartment Story,"[16] which loosely reenacts the wedding scene from the album cover, was a professional production with colorizing and multiple camera angles.*

---

*That said, it was still filmed down the street from Matt and Carin's apartment using friends, family, and Beggars employees as actors.

Backstage at Letterman. (Credit: Sonya Kolowrat)

By the end of the year, *Boxer* would appear in numerous lists ranking the best albums of 2007, including the number one spot in *Paste*, the same magazine that had initially given it a lukewarm review. Without actually mentioning

The National by name, the cover story of *Paste's* year-end issue, teased by a somewhat suspicious photo of the band and Padma lurking in the shadows cast by venetian blinds, read: "These Six Guys Made the Best Record of 2007. Do You Know Who They Are?"[17]

> **Matt Harmon:** Between the records we were selling, the amount of people the band was playing for, and the amount of media attention, everything was rising at the same point. Once we felt it, then we were all like, *Okay, we need to pour some gasoline on this.*

That gas included a major advertising blitz and a specially packaged edition of the CD during the holidays, followed by the joint release of *The Virginia EP* and the *A Skin, A Night* film to coincide with *Boxer's* one year anniversary in 2008. As a result, *Boxer* just kept selling, as did *Alligator* by virtue of people discovering the band. By the end of 2007 *Boxer* had sold 70,000 copies, and continued to move 1,200 copies a week, seemingly on its own.*

> **Sonya Kolowrat:** At some point it became out of our hands. The band reached this point where things just started happening for them, and it didn't matter what we did. It was like they had proven themselves.
> **Roger Trust:** After a year or 18 months, *Boxer* and *Alligator* had combined sales of around a million and

---

*As of the writing of this book, *Boxer* has sold just enough units in the U.S. alone to be certified gold, ever so slightly behind its 2010 successor, *High Violet*.

a vast worldwide fanbase that would anticipate the release of their next album. By then I was convinced that The National was the best band in the world and would become one of its biggest.

*   *   *

15
Signs of Hope and Change

There are several codas to the story of *Boxer*. The most poetic is the happy conclusion to the ballad of Matt and Carin.

> **Matt:** Neither of us liked the idea of weddings. Then Carin got pregnant. We were much more excited about having a kid than we were about getting married.
>
> **Carin:** His mom was like, "You should get married." And then my parents were like, "Yeah, you probably should." We thought it was funny that we were both so surprised our parents cared.
>
> **Matt:** One day we just decided we should get married, and just waltzed towards it together arm in arm.

It was a bluebird day in July, just two months after release, when the couple strolled into the marble chambers of New York City Hall, swore their love to each other before a justice of the peace, and walked back home across the Brooklyn Bridge as man and wife. Soon after they moved into a new apartment, which was followed by the arrival of their daughter Isla. They also quit smoking.

*   *   *

By 2008, The National was a cool band to know, with public figures like Bruce Springsteen and, rather ironically, first daughter Jenna Bush sharing their appreciation.[1] After years of being the band in the sidebar, they were beginning to make headlines of their own. Before their next album they'd get a 4,500-word profile in *The New York Times Magazine*.[2]

In their own world, they were suddenly vital members of the indie scene that was continuing to grow around them. Rather than finally rest on the laurels they'd earned, they wasted no time using their newfound clout to spawn new side projects and collaborations that would eventually become as much a part of their careers as the band itself.

> **Bryce:** *Boxer* was a turning point where we started to know a lot of musicians. In some ways we even became the center of some kind of community.

Demonstrating their newfound connections, the twins began curating what became the 2009 Red Hot charity compilation, *Dark Was the Night*, a massive project epitomizing the indie renaissance of the day with contributions from the likes of Arcade Fire, Beirut, Blonde Redhead, Bon Iver, Cat Power, Conor Oberst, The Decemberists, Dirty Projectors, Feist, Grizzly Bear, Iron & Wine, Spoon, and of course Sufjan Stevens.

Things only escalated on the touring front as well. With The National's growing fanbase empowering them to play bigger concerts in more places, they were finally eating away at the debt they'd accrued since *Sad Songs for Dirty Lovers*.

In the first twelve months of *Boxer* alone, the band notched 139 shows while graduating from tour van to the considerably more comfortable tour bus option. By the time it was over, they'd played 231 shows, including far-flung gigs in Russia and Rio de Janeiro, and a headlining set at the 2009 Pitchfork Music Festival. Add the two years of touring behind *High Violet*, and they managed to squeeze over 450 shows into a five year window.[3]

> **Brandon Reid:** *Alligator* proved they could sell out bars around the world. *Boxer* moved them to theaters and venues. *High Violet* took them to the Albert Hall. And this matters because shows, *not* record sales, are how musicians make money in the 21st century. Period.

While The National had proven they could reliably sell out large rooms by themselves, their most important shows of this era were as the opener for a summer tour with R.E.M. and Modest Mouse. The month-long jaunt, which turned out to be R.E.M.'s final tour, found the band playing massive outdoor amphitheaters for the first time, not to mention Madison Square Garden. By association and by pure exposure, it was a career-altering breakthrough for a band that had relentlessly toured for years in hopes of gaining an audience.

Bryce: R.E.M. was the reason we thought we could be a band. They showed this kind of music can mean something to people. We were very much in their shadow, walking the same path they had taken.

Aaron: Playing these big venues with one of our favorite bands, it felt like we were getting the co-sign, the blessing. It was a special thing.

Just like The Walkmen tour years earlier, the experience also instilled The National with a blueprint for the next stage of their development.

Bryce and Arron looking over their future at Red Rocks. (Credit: Mauricio Carey)

Brandon Reid: It was pretty revealing for everybody to see how someone like R.E.M. did it. Once this situation has been demystified, you're like, *I could do that.* And all of the outdoor venues The National played on that tour, they went on to headline later in their career.

In fact, it was at their June 3 show at Colorado's famed Red Rocks Amphitheater where this very writer, who had been eagerly waiting for the gates to open in order to see Modest Mouse up close, first encountered The National. Like countless other converts on that tour, after witnessing the band's powerful 10-song set, he immediately bought *Boxer* and *Alligator* on vinyl.

* * *

Rewinding to February 2007—just as The National was putting the final touches on *Boxer*—a first-term Illinois senator named Barack Hussein Obama was announcing his longshot bid for the U.S. presidency, lining up behind nationally recognized Democratic figures like Hillary Clinton, Joe Biden, and John Edwards. Fast forward a year and a half later—as the band was wrapping up their run with R.E.M.—Obama had edged out Clinton as their party's presumptive nominee.

Matt: It was exciting when he was rising and becoming the candidate. He was so inspiring.
Lizzy Goodman: He was Kennedy for our generation. There was this sense of deep identification with him

and his story, especially among young people. He was a Black man living in America, and yet he was speaking to us about hope and promise and a future.

That July, the band endorsed Obama's run by selling a T-shirt benefiting the campaign, which juxtaposed his face with the red and blue text "Mr. November."[4] At the same time, their friend Hope Hall, who had co-directed the "Mistaken for Strangers" music video with Matt's brother Tom, had reluctantly fallen into a job as a videographer and filmmaker for the campaign.

> **Hope Hall:** I told them, "I don't know how to make propaganda." And they were like, "That's exactly why you're the right fit!"

Given to her just three weeks before the 2008 Democratic National Convention in Denver, Hope's first assignment for the campaign was daunting. With Obama set to accept the Democratic nomination from the center of Invesco Field—the 74,000-seat home of the Denver Broncos—her task was to create an anthemic video that would introduce the candidate just before he walked onto the stage. With people packed onto the field, capacity was expected to exceed 80,000.

> **Hope Hall:** They basically told me, "We want you to get those 80,000 people on their feet."

With no time to lose, Hope began culling through footage the campaign had produced around the country, sketching out a story about the mass movement of activists and community organizers that Obama was mobilizing. All she needed was an emotive song to soundtrack it.

> **Hope Hall:** I had "Fake Empire" in my head the whole time. The structure of that song made complete sense to me in terms of the narrative.

After getting the band's enthusiastic blessing, Hope took an instrumental version of "Fake Empire" as her base element and began to build her video around its musical movements. Entitled "Signs of Hope and Change," the 2 minute and 40 second piece splices together patriotic images and quotes with a montage of diverse Americans holding actual paper signs that say "HOPE" and "CHANGE."[5] In doing so, Hope reconfigured a world-weary song about existential dread into an uplifting political anthem.

> **Matt:** The music is so uplifting. That's why the song is so great. It sounds like a big victory song, but it's sung about this delusional character who's out drinking and pretending bluebirds are on his shoulder. It's an escapist song set to cinematic victory music.
>
> **Bryce:** I actually wrote "Fake Empire" years before *Boxer*, while backstage in Pensacola, Florida on The Walkmen tour. The music is simple but it has this complex rhythm that I learned from performing with Philip Glass. Matt's lyrics spoke to what was happening in the world politically.
>
> **Lizzy Goodman:** It's sad and hopeful at the same time. The pure emotional experience of how that song feels, it sounds like it comes from darkness but it believes

in a future. Obama's message merged so well with the
emotional resonance of that track.

Matt: Granted, the version they use in the video is
instrumental. I'm not in it at all, which is kind of
damning.

Despite leaving Matt's words out of the video, Hope saw the
song's very title as a comment on American democracy.

Hope Hall: The contradiction between those two
words—"fake" and "empire"—is really important. This
political experiment we are all a part of *is* an empire.
It's our job to come face-to-face with it, deconstruct it,
and continuously put it back together. I think Obama
brought some accessibility to that idea for so many
people.

Then, like *Boxer* itself, Hope's video became its own battle
when, with 10 days until the DNC, she showed it to the
campaign. Their response: the video is great, but there's no
way you can use that song.

Apparently, even though The National had given
wholehearted permission to use "Fake Empire," the
minutiae of campaign finance law dictated that the band
couldn't simply donate the song for free.* This forced the
campaign to license it at a commercial rate, which got the
label and publisher involved, all of whom Hope now had

---

*As part of the process, the band also had to be vetted, with the "Fuck"-
laden and politically open-ended "Mr. November" giving the campaign
some pause.

to convince to make a deal before the fast-approaching convention for which the video had been designed. In true National fashion, everything came down to the last possible moment.

> **Hope Hall:** I was in the motorcade in Denver, as we were driving to the stadium for the speech, still negotiating on a three-way call. On the ground, they were like, "What's the backup? What's the second version?" I was like, "There is no second version! The video was made to the song."

On the night of August 28, minutes before Obama was scheduled to walk out and claim his historic nomination, Hope was filming the man of the hour backstage, nervously wondering whether the last-minute deal had given the production team enough time to include the video. Just as she popped her head out into the open air of the packed stadium, the jumbotron screens went dark for a moment, and the song began to play.

> **Hope Hall:** The stadium got quiet, and then the song builds...and builds...and builds.* At the end everyone got on their feet and started chanting, "YES WE CAN."

"Signs of Hope and Change," and its inseparable soundtrack, had worked. And over the next two months, the video continued to play at Obama's countless campaign rallies,

---

*At this point in the interview, Hope begins crying from emotion.

Obama's speech at the D.N.C., after being warmed up by "Fake Empire." (Credit: Kelly DeLay / CC BY 2.0)

often directly before Mr. Hope-and-Change himself made his big entrance. Then, on the night of November 4, the video was queued up one last time.

It was close to midnight in Chicago's Grant Park, where a mind-boggling crowd of 240,000 estimated supporters had gathered.[6] The erstwhile underdog candidate had just secured the 270 electoral votes needed to become the first African-American Commander-in-Chief in U.S. history. As the emotional mass anxiously waited for the president-elect to emerge and give his victory speech, a familiar off-kilter piano began to blare out of the speakers.[7]

> **Bryce:** I remember getting a text from Will Butler of Arcade Fire, who was in Grant Park when Obama walked out. He was like, "Holy shit! It's 'Fake Empire!'"
>
> **Matt:** To have a little song you write when you're depressed about the world get used like that, it's hard to describe. "Fake Empire" became a part of that story in a tiny way. That's a big part of *Boxer*'s legacy.

Of course The National-Obama story didn't end there. Two years later, the band joined the 44th President on stage for several events rallying support ahead of the 2010 midterms,* and would continue to lend their support at Obama events down the road.

> **Matt:** It was definitely one of those lucky, serendipitous moments that can change everything. That was one of the most exciting things that has ever happened to us, on any level.

Years later, after leaving the White House, Hope got the chance to talk to the now former president, who thanked both her and The National for their help over the years.

> **Hope Hall:** Obama was like, "I just watched that 'Hope and Change' video again! It's like a postcard from

---

*Presumably less familiar with the band than they were with him, the president at one point mistakenly introduced them as "The Nationals."

another time." I was like, "Let me tell you the story about how that video almost never saw the light of day." He was like, "I am *so* glad I never knew about this."

*   *   *

16
That Same Desperate Struggle

A classic album contains multitudes. It presents multiple faces, offers untold interpretations, and grants new experiences each time you come back. It becomes a part of your life.

> **Matt:** I think of the experiences I've had smoking cigarettes and drinking alone while *Blood on the Tracks*, or *Bone Machine*, or *The Boatman's Call* plays over and over again. I think we wanted to make a record that you could just live in. I think that's one of the main reasons why *Boxer* has had such staying power. It's a distinct world.

In perfecting the band's signature sound, *Boxer* invites you in by carving out space between layers of sparring contrasts: Drums versus vocals. Delicate orchestration versus turbulent distortion. The Dessners' tactical songwriting versus the Devendorfs' mystical searching. The agony of Aaron's depressive heartbreak versus the ecstasy of Matt's blossoming love story. The terror of Bush versus the optimism of Obama.

Aaron: It was a record that you could listen to obsessively. And we all did. I think it's our best record in the sense of its cohesiveness. It feels very connected from front to back, even though it goes to different places. "Mistaken for Strangers" and "Green Gloves" are two really different songs, but somehow they live on the same record in a really cool way.

When a band is around as long as The National, is as consistently good as The National, or has as many fans as The National, one album will never be the unanimous favorite. Even the guys in the band can't agree on that. Each record is superior by some measurement, but wherever it sits for you, *Boxer* is close to the top in every category.

Bryce: *Boxer* is a high point of when we managed to pull something off. It's this great creative realization. The whole thing is solid.

*   *   *

Looking back at The National's ongoing career, *Boxer* capped off an incredibly hard-fought and prolific period for the band. In the six years between their debut and *Boxer*, the band released four full-length albums and an EP, each better than the last. Fifteen years and four additional albums later, *Boxer* sits at the heart of their discography, and remains their hardest and most existential work.

Brandon Reid: Coming out of *Alligator* and going into making *Boxer*, you still had a band full of people that had hesitations as to whether this was going to be a sustainable thing. They were still wondering, *Is this what we're doing with our lives? Is this band going to last?*

Scott: It was probably the hardest one to make because of all the circumstances and the expectations we put on ourselves.

Carin: What has really stood out to me, when I look back, is how important it was for the band that the record be good, and just how hard that was.

Matt: What strikes me is how seriously we took it. It felt like this unbelievably stressful, live-or-die challenge. There was deep, deep anxiety over it, and real, real tension over indecision. I'm glad we're not like that anymore.

For a band that entered the ring unsure of whether they had another fight in them, *Boxer's* ultimate success was the difference-maker. By the time it was over, they were touring with rock royalty, soundtracking presidencies, and on a path to releasing Gold-certified and Grammy-winning follow-ups.

Roger Trust: The only way that The National could become the band they did with *High Violet* was to make *Boxer*. It's a watershed album in their development.

Aaron: I felt a lot of hope on the backside of *Boxer*. It's the moment when the forces aligned in the creative process, and we somehow came out with the best record we could have made, maybe even a perfect record. It cemented what we were capable of and gave us a lot of confirmation, both public and private.

Bryan: It kind of marked the end of the beginning, and then the beginning of being a real touring band. Those formative years ended around that time. Whether it was just the natural order of the universe or actually making that specific album, it definitely changed afterwards.

Artistically, The National not only managed to exceed the expectations created by *Alligator*, but subvert them in a way that allowed them to continue evolving.

Bryce: It was a huge leap, the creative expansiveness of it. It wasn't the obvious thing to do after *Alligator*. Our ambitions and unrelenting search for new colors, collaborators, and ideas was rewarded.

Carin: It felt like the beginning of something, because they stretched the canvas so wide. It wasn't a work of art that felt like, *Oh, well now you're pigeonholed and you have to sound like that all the time*. They sounded like a band that could do a lot on their next record.

Boxer also sits not-so coincidentally at the detonation point of when the band's tireless creative energy exploded into an expanding universe of side projects and collaborations with artists as disparate as Taylor Swift, Philip Glass, Justin Vernon, Bob Weir, Booker T. Jones, and Mike Mills.

Brandon Stosuy: If you were to line up The National's discography next to all the side projects, the film projects, the art projects, the one-offs, the festivals

they're curating—there's so much going on at any
time. I feel like *Boxer* gave them that soapbox, and
then they used it really wisely while putting out great
record after great record.

Like any transformative experience, *Boxer* also taught the
band many lessons.

Aaron: We figured out that we have these different gears,
where these fragile, ugly ducklings like "Racing Like a
Pro" are just as important as these big, forceful songs
like "Mistaken for Strangers." *Boxer* really cemented
what the criteria was for finishing a record.

While you could make the case that the long, excruciating
process of creating the album was integral to *Boxer's* success,
and though Peter Katis would remain a vital part of their
process, the band also recognized that paying an hourly rate
in someone else's studio was not going to work for them.

Scott: After the experience of running into the wall
and being in that time-financial-emotional crunch
of finishing the record, we took our earnings from
touring and built a studio in Aaron's garage. We knew
that the way that we work wasn't going to change, but
there was probably a better way to do it.

The constant creative combat of recording also taught them
how to trust and respect each other in the studio.

Matt: Aaron and Bryce and Scott and Bryan and I were
bringing really distinct perspectives and talent, and
we all loved our band. I think that's really what *Boxer*

shows. As much conflict as there was in the making of it, all those things we fought about are what made a good band.

Thomas Bartlett: Working with those guys over the years, it's been a consistent amazement to me how well the albums keep turning out, out of this process that doesn't seem very fun. It's an extraordinary music-making machine constructed of these misfit parts.

In not bending to trends, pressures, or shortcuts, they learned to trust their own instincts.

Peter Katis: The National has had the most slow and steady career ever. There's really no dip or sellout record. They're just doing what they do and they put in so much work. That's pretty incredible.

*   *   *

To become a champion, a boxer needs mental and physical agility, a sixth sense for timing, and an inextinguishable competitive fire.

Brandon Reid: The National have achieved greatness at the altitude that they have because of the severity of the competitiveness inside the band. They're on a journey that's really kind of jet-fueled. They operate at a pace that very few people can keep up with.

Lizzy Goodman: They must on some level still feel that they're always the underdog, which is what makes them rock stars. First it was Interpol, then it was Clap Your Hands Say Yeah. To have that thorn in your side is such a gift, because revenge is one of the primary motivators of great rock and roll.

To remain a champion, a boxer needs a love for the fight, the right team in their corner, and a stubborn insistence to stay standing at all costs. Whether or not you romanticize The National's obstacle-laden road to *Boxer*, their struggle was essential to their long, victorious career.

> **Matt:** *Boxer* is where we all realized that we make our favorite things together. It's fun to think about how we haven't actually changed that much. That same desperate struggle to stay a band is still very much there.

*   *   *

Epilogue

When I first fell in love with The National, sitting 10 rows back from the stage at Red Rocks, I was 17 years old. Despite everyone in the band being twice my age, their music was as relatable as it was interesting and beautiful, speaking to emotions I was feeling then *and* ones I could anticipate feeling in the future.

Nearly 15 years later, *Boxer* is one of those rare albums that has continued to grow with me. After hundreds of spins I never tire of its charms. Knowing that a lot of people have that relationship with *Boxer* was one of my main justifications for proposing a book about it. What I couldn't have expected was how an album that's been with me for almost half my life, has never been more relatable.

While writing this book I was in the first year of my thirties, realizing that my most innocent years were behind me. I was working as a well paid, achingly bored marketing copywriter for a tech company while dreaming of putting my passions to some soul-quenching use. I was in the middle of a global pandemic that overlapped with the last days of the Trump administration. Hardest of all, I was wading through the breakup of my marriage and dealing with the paralyzing realities of depression.

In the process of wrapping my arms around *Boxer*, unlocking its intentions and contextualizing the events surrounding it, things got kind of weird when I found myself projecting myself onto these real and fictional characters and situations.

Through the lyrics I was communing with the guilt I harbor over faded friendships, the self-hatred of being a pseudo-creative corporate sellout, and the humbling awareness of my own uninnocent fall into the unmagnificent lives of adults. In the face of a real-life plague and an even more frightening American presidency, I was finding escapism in music, wine, and homebound isolation. For the first time in my life, I could put myself in Aaron's shoes (as well as other band members who discussed their own depressions and heartbreaks with me) and imagine the pain he was in while writing this music and trying to keep the sadness at bay by obsessing over the work at hand.

The most meta experience of all was uncovering The National's creative journey on *Boxer* while laboring to create my own biggest work to date. I could never have imagined the passion, the torment, the wheel spinning, the moving deadlines, the endless reworking, and all-around exhaustion involved in creating what others will hopefully enjoy as, in their case, 43 minutes of rock music, and, in my case, 33,000 words of rock journalism.

I don't know if my personal experiences make me uniquely qualified to have written this book. What I do know is that my experiences in life and with this album are the opposite of unique. That's what makes *Boxer* such a knockout.

Ryan Pinkard
Spring, 2021

If you were to zoom in, you could see the top half of my head, moments away from discovering The National for the first time. (Credit: Mauricio Carey)

Acknowledgments

First and foremost, thank you to the many people who generously shared their time, memories and perspectives, in some cases for hours on end: Matt Berninger, Aaron Dessner, Bryce Dessner, Scott Devendorf, Bryan Devendorf, Peter Katis, Carin Besser, Alec Hanley Bemis, Brandon Reid, Hope Hall, Brandon Stosuy, Stephen M. Deusner, Lizzy Goodman, Abbey Drucker, Matt Harmon, Sonya Kolowrat, Miwa Okumura, Roger Trust, and Padma Newsome.

Thanks as well to the people who shared photos or granted permission to publish snapshots they forgot about long ago. In addition to numerous individuals above, they include: Mauricio Carey, Mathieu Saura, Graham MacIndoe, Lisa Molinaro, Yun Rhee, and Luke Hughett.

My deepest gratitude to: Tana for being my reader, editor, transcriber, and sounding board. Erik Flannigan, Scott Devendorf (again), Alec Hanley Bemis (again), Brandon Reid (again), Shaun Gibson, and Jamie Heaslip for opening so many doors. Bryan Devendorf (again) for dusting off his red pen just for me. Leah Babb-Rosenfeld, Rachel Moore, boice-Terrel Allen, and Joseph Gautham for helping me turn a proposal into a manuscript into a book. Josh, Claudia,

Tusse, Jamie, and Linda for regularly cheering me on. Dejlig for keeping me company. Mom and Dad for everything. Mogens for showing me Tom Waits, Leonard Cohen, and Lou Reed. Nick and Jack for that day at Red Rocks. My old pals at TIDAL who unlocked countless experiences and opportunities. And to Old Grand-Dad and Old Overholt whiskeys for spicing up many a late-night hot toddy.

Above all, thank you to The National for creating this perfect, endlessly explorable album, and for adding so much beauty and feeling to the world. This book is dedicated to you and all your hard-earned fans.

Notes

Chapter 1

1   Jason Killingsworth, "The National: Grow Up! Look Sharp! Be Responsible!" *Paste Magazine*, November 27, 2007, www .pastemagazine.com/music/the-national/.

2   Sam Sodomsky, "The National Are a Band of Brothers—But Not Like Oasis" *Pitchfork*, September 21, 2017, https://pitchfork .com/features/family-matters/the-national-are-a-band-of -brothersbut-not-like-oasis/.

3   "Project Nim," January 25, 1999, https://web.archive.org/web /19990125102415/ http://www.projectnim.com/.

4   Katie Skibinski, "Project Nim," *Columbia Spectator Archive*, March 26, 1998, http://spectatorarchive.library.columbia.edu/?a =d&d=cs19980326-02.2.12&.

5   Brandon Stosuy, "Have You Heard the National Guitar?" *Artvoice*, https://brassland.org/releases/the-national.

6   Jason Nickey, "The National: The National," *Pitchfork*, October 14, 2001, https://pitchfork.com/reviews/albums/5717-the -national/.

Chapter 2

1   Michael D. Ayers, "The National Is Uncomfortably Fun," *The Village Voice,* May 11, 2010, https://www.villagevoice.com/2010 /05/11/the-national-is-uncomfortably-fun/.

2   Brandon Stosuy, "The National: Sad Songs for Dirty Lovers," *Pitchfork*, October 14, 2003, https://pitchfork.com/reviews/ albums/5718-sad-songs-for-dirty-lovers/.

3   Will Welch, "Local Talent: The National Write Emotions," *The Fader Magazine*, November, 2003, 90.

4   Greg Kot, "The National: Sad Songs for Dirty Lovers," *Rolling Stone,* October 30, 2003, 88.

5   Hamish McBain, "The National Sad Songs for Dirty Lovers: Bad Seeds of the Big Apple," *NME,* November 1, 2003.

6   David Peschek, "State of Grace," *Uncut*, December, 2003.

Chapter 3

1   https://www.setlist.fm/.

2   "The National Daytrotter Session," *Paste Magazine,* July 9, 2007, https://www.pastemagazine.com/noisetrade/music/the -national/jul-9-2007-daytrotter-studio-rock-island-il.

3   https://www.youtube.com/user/yrhee/videos.

4   Bayon, "La fibre National," *Libération*, May 26, 2003.

5   "The National: The Black Sessions," *Music Is Art,* December 29, 2013, https://www.musicisartmag.com/the-national-black -session/.

Chapter 5

1 Joe Tangari, "The National: Alligator," *Pitchfork*, April 4, 2005, https://pitchfork.com/reviews/albums/5719-alligator/.

2 "Alligator," *Billboard*, April 16, 2005, https://www.billboard.com/articles/news/63351/alligator/.

3 Christian Hoard, "Alligator," *Rolling Stone*, April 21, 2005, https://www.rollingstone.com/music/music-album-reviews/alligator-187268/.

4 Rob Hughes, "The National," *Uncut,* May 15, 2006, https://web.archive.org/web/20060515202406/ https://www.uncut.co.uk/music/the_national/reviews/8601.

5 "American Mary Press," American Mary, February 8, 2006, https://web.archive.org/web/20060208014105/ http://www.americanmary.com/press/uncutalbumsofyear2005.jpg.

6 Mojo, May, 2005, 108, https://www.metacritic.com/music/alligator/the-national/critic-reviews.

7 "The National Alligator," *E! Online,* April 21, 2006, https://web.archive.org/web/20060421054726/ https://www.eonline.com/reviews/facts/music/revid/0,1107,3611,00.html.

Chapter 6

1 Nick Routley, "Visualizing 40 Years of Music Industry Sales," *Visual Capitalist*, October 6, 2018, https://www.visualcapitalist.com/music-industry-sales/.

2 https://www.setlist.fm/.

3 Brian Howe, "Clap Your Hands Say Yeah," *Pitchfork*, June 21, 2005, https://pitchfork.com/reviews/albums/1811-clap-your -hands-say-yeah/.

4 "Clap Your Hands Say No," *PopMatters*, June 2, 2006, https:// www.popmatters.com/clap-your-hands-say-yeah-060602 -2496107893.html.

5 Stephen M. Deusner, "The National/Clap Your Hands Say Yeah," *Pitchfork*, September 19, 2005, https://pitchfork.com/ features/article/6146-the-national-clap-your-hands-say-yeah/.

6 "The National, Clap Your Hands Say Yeah / Sept. 23, 2005 / Chicago (Schuba's)," *Billboard*, September 27, 2005, https:// www.billboard.com/articles/news/61305/the-national-clap -your-hands-say-yeah-sept-23-2005-chicago-schubas.

7 Adrian Mack, "Clap Your Hands Say Yeah," *Straight .com*, October 6, 2005, https://web.archive.org/web /20090530011807/ https://www.straight.com/article/clap-your -hands-say-yeah.

8 "I Stayed for the National - 2005 Plug Award Winners," *Brooklyn Vegan*, February 3, 2006, https://www.brooklynvegan .com/i-stayed-for-th-1/.

9 "American Mary Weather," Website, April 9, 2006, https://web .archive.org/web/20060409085146/ http://www.americanmary .com/weather/.

Chapter 7

1 Mark Morgenstein, "The National's Anthems," *CNN Entertainment*, October 25, 2010, https://www.cnn.com/2010/ SHOWBIZ/Music/10/18/the.national.tour/index.html.

Chapter 8

1   John Cheever, "The Swimmer" in *The Stories of John Cheever* (New York: Alfred A. Knopf, 1978), 713–725.

Chapter 11

1   *A Skin, A Night*, directed by Vincent Moon, (2008).

2   Tom Milway, "The National: 'We nearly lost our minds making Boxer,'" *Drowned in Sound*, December 11, 2007, https://drownedinsound.com/in_depth/2684085-the-national--we-nearly-lost-our-minds-making-boxer.

Chapter 12

1   Christopher Hooton, *Coffee and Flowers*, podcast audio, Coffee and Flowers podcast, 2019, https://coffeeandflowers.podbean.com/.

Chapter 14

1   Dave Maher, "The National Enter the Ring with Boxer," *Pitchfork*, February 26, 2007, https://web.archive.org/web/20081218045144/ http://www.pitchforkmedia.com/article/news/41400-exclusive-the-national-enter-the-ring-with-boxer.

2   "Pulse Music," Pulse Music, March 8, 2007, https://pulsemusic.proboards.com/thread/54609/national-boxer-22-top-juggernaut.

3   "New National - 'Fake Empire,'" *Stereogum.com*, March 22, 2007, https://web.archive.org/web/20070331084203/ https://www.stereogum.com/archives/004905.html.

4   "The National's 'Boxer' Has Leaked," *Sixeyes*, March 31, 2007, http://sixeyes.blogspot.com/2007/03/nationals-boxer-has-leaked.html.

5   "Premature Evaluation: The National - Boxer," *Stereogum.com*, April 3, 2007, https://web.archive.org/web/20070520083214/http://www.stereogum.com/archives/premature-evaluation/the-national-boxer.html.

6   Brandon Stosuy, "Quit Your Day Job: The National," *Stereogum.com*, April 4, 2007, https://web.archive.org/web/20070516011318/ https://www.stereogum.com/archives/005014.html.

7   4AD, "The National - Mistaken for Strangers," 4AD, May 8, 2007, https://www.youtube.com/watch?v=cgRsYkKb1eI.

8   "The National - Five Nights at Bowery Sold Out, Opening for Arcade Fire, South Street Seaport," *Brooklyn Vegan*, April 18, 2007, https://www.brooklynvegan.com/the-national-fi/.

9   Rob Sheffield, "Boxer," *Rolling Stone*, May 14, 2007, https://www.rollingstone.com/music/music-album-reviews/boxer-99444/.

10 Jon Pareles, "Critics' Choice New CD's," *The New York Times*, May 21, 2007, https://www.nytimes.com/2007/05/21/arts/music/21choi.html?ref=music&pagewanted=all.

11 Jeff Leven, "The National - Boxer," *Paste Magazine*, May 21, 2007, https://www.pastemagazine.com/music/the-national-boxer/.

12 David Peschek, "The National, Boxer," *The Guardian*, May 17, 2007, https://www.theguardian.com/music/2007/may/18/popandrock.shopping5.

13 Stephen M. Deusner, "The National Boxer," *Pitchfork,* May 21, 2007, https://pitchfork.com/reviews/albums/10242-boxer/.

14 "Billboard 200 Week of June 9, 2007," *Billboard*, June 9, 2007, https://www.billboard.com/charts/billboard-200/2007-06-09.

15 "The National on Letterman - July 24, 2007," July 25, 2007, https://www.youtube.com/watch?v=NBujZr20O6M.

16 4AD, "The National - 'Apartment Story,' 4AD, October 9, 2007, https://www.youtube.com/watch?v=S97xQKZDV_4.

17 "Paste Magazine," December 2007-January 2008, Issue #38, cover.

Chapter 15

1 "The Boss and Ms. Bush Approve of the National," *Brassland,* March 7, 2008, https://brassland.org/news/the-boss-and-ms-bush-approve-of-the-national.

2 Nicholas Dawidoff, "The National Agenda," *New York Times*, April 23, 2010, https://www.nytimes.com/2010/04/25/magazine/25national-t.html?pagewanted=all.

3 https://www.setlist.fm/.

4 "The National + Barack Obama," Commotion, July 8, 2008, https://commotionmag.wordpress.com/2008/07/08/the-national-barack-obama-t-shirt/.

5   "Signs of Hope & Change," September 1, 2008, https://www
    .youtube.com/watch?v=EcRA2AZsR2Q.

6   Monica Davey, "Celebrating Obama in Grant Park," *New York
    Times*, November 5, 2008, https://thecaucus.blogs.nytimes.com
    /2008/11/05/waiting-for-obama-in-grant-park/.

7   "Election Night 2008 - Barack Obama wins in Grant Park,"
    October 13, 2009, https://www.youtube.com/watch?v
    =04ALIKUWGrI.

Also Available in the Series

ALSO AVAILABLE IN THE SERIES

ALSO AVAILABLE IN THE SERIES

ALSO AVAILABLE IN THE SERIES